D0955896

The Evolved Eater

The
Evolved
Eater

A Quest to Eat Better,
Live Better, and Change the World

Nick Taranto

St. Martin's Press New York

www.stmartins.com

Charts and graphs by Daphne Taranto

Designed by Patrice Sheridan
Interior fruit and vegetable photos by Sailorr, Courtesy of Shutterstock

The Library of Congress Cataloging-in-Publication Data is available upon request.

ISBN 978-1-250-12211-7 (hardcover)
ISBN 978-1-250-12212-4 (ebook)

Our books may be purchased in bulk for promotional, educational, or business use. Please contact your local bookseller or the Macmillan Corporate and Premium Sales Department at 1-800-221-7945, extension 5442, or by email at MacmillanSpecialMarkets@macmillan.com.

First Edition: March 2018

10 9 8 7 6 5 4 3 2 1

For Nimmi, my partner in crime,

who keeps my eyes on the stars

and my feet on the ground

Contents

Acknowledgments

It's hard to run a business, and it's hard to write a book. Doing both at the same time is nearly impossible—without a team of fantastic people. I want to thank my mom and dad for their genes, guidance, and funny memories. Bree Barton for her research, writing, and desert and dessert tales. Carlye Adler for her edits, strategy, and "personal training." Nicole Sinno for her research and "product management." My agent, Anthony Mattero, for believing in me and making magic happen. Elizabeth Beier at St. Martin's Press for her visions and revisions. My sisters, Alice and Daphne, for their design prowess and funny captions. And the entire #TeamPlated for an incredible journey since 2012. As Ken Blanchard said, "None of us is as smart as all of us." Let's go!

Author's Note

I started working on this book in 2015. At the time, I remember thinking that the food industry was already moving at breakneck pace, changing and morphing seemingly every week, if not every day. That's a big part of why I wanted to write a book—to capture and share my front-row perspective on an industry in the midst of disruption.

Wow. If I thought things were crazy in 2015, then they have become legitimately bonkers since then. Billions of dollars poured into the food technology space, and "meal kits" became a household term. Amazon bought Whole Foods. Our closest competitor went public and had one of the worst Initial Public Offerings in recent memory. And we were acquired for hundreds of millions of dollars by Albertsons, one of the largest grocery stores in the United States.

As you'll read over the coming pages, my cofounder and I started Plated because we had a vision: We believed we could use data and technology to make healthy, affordable, and delicious food a reality for everyone.

Building a business from scratch is really, really, really hard. We faced rejection and bankruptcy and naysayers every day for years on end. But we fought through. And while the journey is nowhere close to over, we are winning.

Albertsons is the parent company of nineteen grocery banners, including Vons, Safeway, Shaws, Jewel Osco, Pavilions, and Acme. If you have spent any time in the United States, chances are you've shopped at a store run by Albertsons. Albertsons owns the biggest certified USDA organic brand in the country and welcomes 35 million weekly shoppers in over 2,300 stores. The scale, and the opportunity for Plated to accelerate our vision, is massive. As you read the pages that follow here, I hope you become as excited as we are!

I wrote this book for smart, passionate, hungry, busy readers. If you're like me, you're trying to squeeze this book in between a dozen other activities, and you want to learn something, but you also want the time you commit here to be fun, or at least entertaining. I have always thought that footnotes get in the way of fun. Instead, I decided to use endnotes. I have meticulously sourced, and if you want to get more background or go deeper on any subject, the endnotes are there for you. If you'd rather get going and keep cruising, then let me get out of your way!

The Evolved Eater

Introduction

Toward a Better Food Future

At Plated, we are on a mission to feed ten billion people in a healthy, affordable, and delicious way. Thanks for picking up this book and taking the time to hear a bit more about what we've done, what we have planned, and why we believe it matters. I'm going to cover a lot of ground here as quickly and efficiently as I can while still having fun, so buckle up, and let's get started!

Toward a Better Food Future

When we started Plated in early 2012, I was twenty-seven years old, recently married, and fresh out of the Marine Corps. I moved back to New York City, started working on Wall Street, and put on twenty pounds in under six months. I was pasty, overweight, and depressed—and I knew there had to be a better way to eat (and live). That's when a business school buddy and I teamed up to create a solution.

Our vision was to use technology and data to create a world where healthy, affordable, and delicious food is available for everyone. As business school guys who were excited about using technology to solve big problems, we saw an enormous market opportunity. In 2012, more than 30 percent of all electronics were bought online, but less than 2 percent of food in the United States came through e-commerce. As outsiders to the food industry, we saw the opportunity to build a large, profitable, mission-driven company that made good eating easier for tens of millions of people.

After studying the food industry and deep-diving on where we were falling short on food in our own lives, we realized this:

> Eating fresh, real food is the best way to both connect to where your food is coming from and to ensure that you and your family are eating only high-quality, sustainable, healthy ingredients.

When we started Plated, here's what we were thinking: The future of food will be defined by a return to freshness and quality. Increasingly more people now realize that what we eat has an impact on our health and the health of the planet. In order to keep up with the demands of both consumers and the planet, we have to embrace new technologies and growing methods. While the pastoral notion of farming and food will always exist, a greater willingness to accept technology and innovation into that picture is also needed. And we wanted to push the vanguard.

Five years later, Plated has delivered tens of millions of meals and chef-designed recipes across the United States (we deliver to the entire Lower 48), we merged with one of the country's largest grocers, we employ hundreds of people in multiple locations—and it feels like we are just getting started. We have also ignited a dialogue about where we are, where we want to go together, and what this means for the future of food in a quest to change how we eat in this country—and around the world.

Today at Plated, we deliver everything you need to cook a delicious dinner at home in about thirty minutes. We believe that deciding what to do for dinner shouldn't be a struggle and that convenience shouldn't come at the cost of deliciousness. We deliver the ingredients you need, when and where you want them, precisely measured for the recipes you've chosen. That means less prep time, less food waste, and more control over your schedule—and your life.

What we figured out, and why our business model works better than traditional food models, is that consumers crave choice, quality, convenience, and flavor—and that they're not willing to compromise. In the age of instant transportation, digital dating, and connected everything, the traditional food industry has not kept up or innovated fast enough to meet consumers where they need us. The consequences of this inability to evolve have had a negative impact on all of us.

Why does good, fresh food have to be more expensive? Why does healthy, nutritious food that is grown sustainably only need to be for the rich? High-quality, nutritious food should be the right of every person. And that is why eventually, hopefully not that long from now, we want Plated to be for everyone. We need to first prove that a good business model that delivers good food can also deliver good profits and returns to investors. There are still many haters out there who don't think it's possible, but give us a few years to prove them wrong.

For most of my personal evolution, I didn't know much about the source of our national eating disorder or what it would take to fix it. I've lived many different chapters in my thirty-two years. I am a husband and "cofounder" of two little girls. I am an Ironman triathlete and a recovering ultramarathon runner. I received my MBA from Harvard. I was a Marine Corps infantry officer, and I worked on Wall Street—albeit briefly. And now I am passionate about building a business that can make good food a reality for billions of people.

But I haven't always been that way. This book will chronicle my own journey from a young dude who hustled Halloween candy to someone who genuinely cares about what we eat and where it comes from—and is doing something about it.

I hope this book serves as a call to arms. While much about food has improved over the last two decades, we are still facing a crisis. The most food-abundant nation in human history has gotten good eating horribly wrong—but it's on each one of us to help fix both what and how we eat.

At Plated, we're still in the early days of our evolution, just as my own path to become an Evolved Eater continues to unfold. We are stoked about the meal kit business we are building today, and we acknowledge that the challenges and opportunities that lie ahead of us are massive. The fundamental problem is that Big Food built a business model and food system that no longer works. Our solution needs to be building from the ground up a new and better system for delivering fresh food, where data and technology power everything. Big Food focused on convenience to the exclusion of connection and experience. Our business model harnesses technology to reconnect people to both their food and the experience of preparing and sharing it.

The traditional food companies' solution to feeding three billion incremental mouths across the planet is more riskily altered, highly processed products. As I started my research for this book, I came up with an acronym for these cheap and dangerous products: CRAP (Consumable Riskily Altered Provisions). I define CRAP as foods that have been chemically processed and made solely or mainly from refined ingredients and artificial substances.

The chairman of the world's biggest food company, Nestlé, recently went on record to say, "Nature is not good to human beings."[1] Peter Brabeck-Letmathe views food as a thing to be artificially designed in order to deliver optimal convenience at the lowest possible cost.

For those of us who are spending our careers creating access to simple, real, minimally processed food straight from the farm (whether it be traditional, hydroponic, or vertical), Nestlé's perspective challenges the idea that real food can supply humans with all the things we need to live long, productive, happy, and healthy lives. Nestlé argues that further processing and fortifying is the only way to feed humanity.[2] But as we will see, this is nothing more than what I call the CRAP Trap: Big Food's hyperprocessed business model that prioritizes low-cost convenience over our health and happiness.

This Big Food point of view is diametrically opposed to how we think about the future of food at Plated. As we will see, we are fooling ourselves if we think that the future of nutrition science is already upon us. By processing and tinkering with foods, we adulterate them and turn them into something insidious. We believe that *someday* nutrition science *may* be at a place where food engineering delivers healthy and delicious results, but that day is not here today. And until that day arrives, we believe that working to make fresh, delicious, and real food as affordable and accessible as possible is the only path forward.

Ten years from now, Plated will have evolved radically and grown exponentially, and we will be serving needs and markets that we can't yet even imagine. Right now, we are working on something big and important: dinner. We'll delight millions of customers, every week, and in the process, we will build a big, profitable business.

We believe this focus is key to our success. Many more start-ups have died from drowning in opportunity than have died from starving of focus. It's impossible to predict the future, but if we succeed in our mission, one thing is certain: We will expand beyond cooking, we will expand beyond dinner, and we will expand to serve hundreds of millions and eventually billions of people, making it easier for them to eat better. And this success will be driven by building a robust, healthy, and profitable business.

Eating is one of the most fundamental parts of being human.

Yet, as a well-educated, fitness-obsessed person, prior to starting Plated, I knew surprisingly little about what I should be eating. During my time as a marine, I had choked down MREs (meals ready to eat). I was with the world's best fighting force, being pushed to the limit to serve my country, and we were getting 100 percent of our calories for weeks on end from a potent mix of riskily altered provisions.

When I got off active duty and made my way back to New York, it seemed like everywhere I looked there was a new set of nutritional guidance or dieting advice. None of it was helpful or sustainable. Like so many things in America, food was abundant—endless fast-food chains, overloaded supermarkets, and cacophonous marketing shouting everywhere.

But here's the shocking part: Every year, more people in the United States die from diet-related diseases like diabetes than have died during the entire global war on terror. Sickeningly, at the same time, one in five kids in this country goes to bed hungry. And even as a well-educated person, I had no idea how or what I was supposed to eat.

I was overweight, unhappy, and scared that I was on a path to obesity and diabetes, like much of my family. One day when I looked in the mirror, the person I saw was a stranger to me. When my wife got me a colon cleanse for my birthday, I knew things had gone too far.

Eating is arguably the most important human activity. But eating in the twenty-first century has become overly complicated. Most of us have come to rely on experts and labels (*all-natural, paleo, gluten-free, low-carb, organic*) to tell us what, when, and how to eat. The pronouncements of doctors, diet-book authors, media pundits, the U.S. government, and nutrition pseudoscientists create an inescapable confusion. Every day, we are inundated with information, yet the average American citizen still doesn't know what or how he or she should be eating. And for those of us who do know, turning that understanding into reality is fraught with complexity. The problem is not what you don't know—the problem is what you think you know that is wrong.

Trust me, I used to be that guy.

Surprisingly, the more time I spent researching and thinking about how to eat better, the simpler the solution became. I learned that nutrition science is still very primitive. In the words of Michael Pollan, one of the preeminent food writers of our age, nutrition science "is today approximately where surgery was in the year 1650— very promising, and very interesting to watch, but are you ready to let them operate on you?"[3]

As Josh Hix (my Plated cofounder) and I began digging more deeply into the food industry, what we saw both horrified and excited us. Food is one of the biggest industries in the world (more than $1 trillion in annual consumption in the United States alone) but it is surprisingly troglodytic. That's a fancy word for a system that is inefficient, ugly, and unevolved. Picture a prehistoric crustacean bungling around a murky pool of water—not a creature you'd want to trust for your health and happiness.

I wrote this book to push how you think about the food you consume and the industry that produces it. I hope this book helps you make more informed choices about what and how you eat, and I hope it inspires you to look toward a better food future and actively work with us to make it become reality.

Our mission at Plated is to create a world where healthy, affordable, and delicious food is available for everyone. This is a book about why and how we are going to use data and technology to feed ten billion people "the Plated Way."

Spoiler alert. Here is one of my big conclusions: New food ideas require new food companies. Big Food is not going to feed ten billion people the way they need to be fed. And we are not going to do this on our own—this is a huge challenge and a daunting mission. And we need your help.

How This Book Is Organized

APPETIZER
My Journey from Junk-Food Junkie
to Evolved Eater

I'll briefly talk through my own food history from candy hustler to consuming thousands of calories during solitary eighteen-hour ultramarathons in the mountains to slurping whale blubber in the Arctic to Marine Corps MREs and Wall Street pad Thai takeout—and how I didn't find happiness until I began my own journey to become an Evolved Eater. Along the way, that chubby, clueless kid I used to be experienced an epiphany: What we eat matters. A lot.

FIRST COURSE
The Story of Humans and Food:
How We Got to This Place Where Food Is a
Problem Instead of a Solution

How did we get to this place where food is a problem instead of a solution for most of the world? How did we get so disconnected from our kitchens and our food?

In chapter 1, I'll outline the problems, and we'll come to understand that there is a massive drawback to how we eat as modern Americans. In chapter 2, we'll go back three million years in history, and we will explore how human evolution has a direct impact on why we cook and why we've compromised for the CRAP Trap. In chapter 3, we pick up with the end of the Second World War, when Big Food began replacing our cooking traditions with manufactured riskily altered provisions.

SECOND COURSE
The Plated Mission: Why a New Form of Food Production and Distribution Is Necessary If We Are Going to Reconnect with Our Food

In the next four chapters, we will explore exactly how Big Food changed our food world. In chapter 4, we will look into the way food is grown, produced, and manufactured in the United States and why that process is making us sick. I take a trip to my family farm in South Dakota, and I contrast that experience to how technology is changing the face of modern food production. In chapter 5, we will explore why processed provisions are so much more attractive and addictive, both to us as consumers and Big Food from a business model perspective. In chapter 6, we will walk through the cacophony of confusion that is created through modern food marketing and how that hurts us and our children. And in chapter 7, we will dive into the nascent world of nutrition science and the future of the quantified self. I bleed, I pee, and I poop in an obsessive effort to understand what I should be eating.

THIRD COURSE
How to Feed Ten Billion People

But don't give up all hope quite yet. In chapter 8, I'll talk about how and why we started Plated to do things differently from Big Food and escape the CRAP Trap. In chapter 9, we'll discuss the future of food and nutrition and what we can do to save both our waistlines and the planet. In chapter 10, we'll talk about cooking and happiness. And in the conclusion, I'll share some very practical things that you can do to make a change, starting right now.

Becoming an Evolved Eater is not a destination but a journey. My personal path to transforming into an Evolved Eater was catalyzed by starting Plated, and just as I have evolved to meet new challenges and demands, so has Plated.

New Food Ideas Require New Food Companies

How do we fight the millions of years of human evolution that sit on our shoulders, and in our guts, that are pushing us toward riskily altered foods? How do we encourage healthier habits on the whole so that our diet is more heavily tilted toward fresher foods and smaller portions?

We need to change our memories and associations so that our taste preferences change over time, so that we crave roasted sweet potatoes instead of potato chips.

Sound crazy?

The really crazy part is that the way our food system is currently configured is making us sick. Fixing it is only possible through making the healthy, real, delicious foods the default through easier access and education. And that's what Plated is all about.

Here are four core beliefs that Josh and I had that have come to define how we are building Plated to be a brand and business that will last for decades:

Belief 1: Transparency and control over personal and
    planetary health are essential.
Belief 2: The definition of healthy living is intensely
    personal.
Belief 3: People succeed when it's easier to do the right
    thing than the wrong thing.
Belief 4: Food, and the experiences of choosing it,

cooking it, and sharing it, are to be celebrated, and
thoughtful design in all things is an essential part of
that celebration.

I'll expand on these beliefs in the chapters to come because they
form the basis of how we think about building a better food business and a better food system.

How do we evolve the food system forward so that it helps our
planet and our bodies while still being a very pleasurable experience?
It's deceptively alluring to say that Evolved Eaters need to hit Pause
and go back in time to an earlier, less-industrialized era. "Let's throw
away this system and go back to a simpler world! Let's harvest our
own kale and beans and cook every meal of the day!" But peel back
one layer of the onion, and that solution fails the sniff test. In a survey conducted in 2012, over half of Americans claimed ignorance.
Working out their income tax, they said, was easier than knowing
how to eat well.[4]

What does it mean to be an Evolved Eater?

You don't have to grow your own food, religiously practice
veganism, and be a walking encyclopedia of nutrition. Food in the
twenty-first century has become complicated, complex, and overwhelming, and as we'll see later, when things get complicated, we
often fail. Eating doesn't need to be complicated or painful or over-
thought, and that's what the Evolved Eater revolution is all about.

I've found that more evolved eating has made me feel better, look
better, and have a better life. I've learned that what I eat has a direct impact on how I feel. I've learned that preparing meals with
the people I love offers an unparalleled opportunity for greater
health, happiness, and connection. And while nutrition science is
still a nebulous no-man's-land, I've learned that cooking more really
does lead to living better. I'm on my way to becoming an Evolved
Eater—and I'm not alone.

Several years ago, after we appeared on the hit TV show *Shark Tank*, Josh and I were concerned that we had tapped out the market for our cook-at-home delivery service. We had several tens of thousands of customers, and we were worried that there just weren't that many more potential people to serve. Neither of us comes from a traditional marketing background, but we worked with some supersmart folks to conduct proprietary market research asking questions like "How big can this market be?" "How many customers are out there?" "What do they look like, and how do they live their lives?"

What came back formed the genesis of this book. More than thirty-one million Americans are Evolved Eaters, conscientious consumers who care about what they eat and where it comes from. Evolved Eaters value connection, discovery, integrity, ambition, and balance. They're the kind of people who strive constantly to improve, and eating is an inseparable part of this evolution. They want quality and value in every bite of their lives.

Evolved Eaters are curious, ambitious, highly connected individuals. They want good food and good information. They are men and women from all walks of life who share one common trait: They are voracious for a better way to eat. While eventually we want our business model to work for *everyone*, today we are building the Plated brand for Evolved Eaters. An Evolved Eater is, by definition, an evolving eater, and when you need us along the way, we'll be there for you.

If the population continues to grow as predicted, and if the way food is grown, manufactured, distributed, marketed, purchased, and consumed doesn't change, what we can expect is increasingly more riskily altered, heavily processed, food-like products. One solution to feeding three billion incremental mouths across the planet is a more consumer-friendly version of MREs. Imagine shelf-stable jalapeño cheese spread, heat-and-eat chili, and rib-shaped pork-substitute patties for breakfast, lunch, and dinner—forever. There is a contingent in both Silicon Valley and the more established food world who believe that tasteless shakes and synthetic, lab-designed nutrition is the answer. Trust me, this is not a palatable future. For anyone.

The solution must rise from a new breed of food companies focused on making real, good, fresh food more affordable and accessible. Big Food doesn't have the answers, and it is not capable of developing the answers on its own. If we are going to feed the world and do it affordably, conveniently, and in a sustainable, healthy, and delicious way, then the answer must come from technology and data-driven companies like Plated. We can prove that good food can be grown in a good way, affordably, where workers are treated well, and where the earth, our waistlines, our wallets, and our relationships don't pay the price.

The food supply chain (a farm at one end and a meal at the other) isn't really a "chain." As described in chapter 3, the food supply chain is actually more like a food pyramid, at least the way it exists today: The fast-food joints sit at the top, supplied by the processors and manufacturers, who get their raw inputs from meat producers and farmers, who form the base of the pyramid.[5]

And over time, this is how I came to understand that eating and farming are the same thing. We are fooling ourselves if we believe that we can build a sustainable, healthy, affordable, and convenient approach to food on the base of what currently exists. We can't think about changing only parts of the way we eat; that is too short-sighted and narrow-minded. We need to build an entirely new and better way to eat, where fresh and real food is a reality for everyone.[6]

There is so much work to be done that it's easy to get overwhelmed, but in this book and in my life in general, I try to be a cheerleader for action. Instead of fretting about the future of food and preaching to the artisanal-cocktail kale-encrusted choir, my hope is that this book is a call to arms that leads you to do something different.

That shouldn't be scary. For example, one of my top pieces of advice is *learn to be a hedonist*. It is very possible to train yourself to love cooking and to experience deep levels of satisfaction, happiness, and pleasure from the act. If I could do it, anyone can. This doesn't mean you need to perpetually wear an apron and reek of sautéed shallots, but it does mean developing real-life solutions for staying close to your food and eating *better*—not just healthier, tastier, or more conveniently.

At Plated, we have come a remarkably long way in just a few years. But the challenges we have already overcome (getting our business up and off the ground, avoiding bankruptcy, and figuring out how to do right by our customers, our investors, our employees, and the environment) are small compared to the challenges we still have ahead of us. We are up against some of the biggest problems that have defined the modern world. In order to succeed in our mission, we need your help.

Just like Darwin's theory of evolution, Big Food's evolution thus far has not been deliberate. Monkeys and turtles don't sit there planning how they will adapt to changing times—they just react and either survive or die. We see similar behavior from the world's biggest food companies—they are the result of a process that was not necessarily consciously constructed.

The intersection of my personal quest, Plated's journey, the history of modern food, and human evolution come together over the following pages. These disparate threads all share the common theme of unintended consequences, some good, some bad. Darwin's theory doesn't have a goal beyond survival. At Plated, we now have the opportunity to consciously evolve. I hope you'll come with me!

Picture of an Evolved Eater

Jordan Burns, Washington, D.C.

Jordan is a student at American University, and she wrote this note and sent it to the Plated Customer Care Team: 21 Reasons Why Plated Changed My Life[7]

Here are 21 reasons why Plated has changed who I am today:

1. I no longer eat frozen food every night.

2. My relationship with my mom has gotten stronger.

3. I know how to make a basic dinner into a real meal.

4. Trying new things doesn't scare me anymore.

5. I understand servings now.

6. My boyfriend and I have another way to bond.

7. I realized I have been using way too much oil.

8. I don't second-guess myself in the kitchen anymore.

9. I have come to appreciate the art of timing.

10. I realize now how hard it must have been for my mom to cook dinner for six kids every night.

11. I can finally go to the grocery store and not just buy junk food.

12. Herbs and spices aren't just an afterthought.

13. I don't feel the need to constantly go out to dinner.

14. I have something to look forward to in the mail every week.

15. I have become obsessed with kitchen utensils.

16. I have figured out that there is so much more than just mild cheddar cheese.

17. Multiple steps in a recipe no longer make me recoil.

(continued)

18. The microwave is no longer my most-used kitchen appliance.

19. I have become mindful while eating.

20. I spend a lot more time discussing food now.

21. I learned that cooking isn't a task, it's an experience.

Appetizer

My Journey from Junk-Food Junkie to Evolved Eater

Confessions of a Candy Hustler

Plated isn't my first foray into the food business. I had a very successful candy business when I was a kid. And by "very successful," I mean I got shut down by the cops on my first day. That's right. What follows are the confessions of a second-grade candy hustler.

I grew up in a leafy suburb of New York City, the eldest of four kids. I was lucky in many ways—I walked to my elementary school and played with the neighborhood kids at the park down the street. Both of my parents worked. My mom was a pediatrician, and my dad took the train into the city every day to work as a health care consultant. He worked long hours, and we didn't see him much during the week, but we spent a lot of time together on the weekends.

Both he and my mom loved to cook, and they made family—and family meals—a priority.

But don't get me wrong—I wasn't some kind of kindergarten health nut slurping down chia-and-spinach shakes. I was a chubby little kid. I loved to eat, and I really didn't care what I was eating or where it came from. One Halloween, when I was eight years old, I went trick-or-treating with a giant Hefty garbage bag. When I got home that night, the bag was *packed* with hundreds, if not thousands, of pieces of candy.

Of course at the time, I had no idea that candy was riskily altered food, full of empty calories and processed chemicals I couldn't pronounce. All I knew was that I wanted to eat it, and nobody was going to come between my pudgy little fingers and my candy. You can imagine my surprise when my mom said, "Nick, you can keep ten pieces and you can put ten more in the freezer, but you have to either throw away the rest or give it to the other kids."

This was totally unacceptable. "I don't want to give it away," I said. "I want to eat it."

"You can't eat it."

"*Fine.*"

What my mom didn't know was that by her toeing a hard line on the Halloween candy, she was actually instilling in me my very first entrepreneurial aspirations. No way was I going to throw that candy away. If she wouldn't let me eat it, then I was going to sell it.

In the early 1990s, computers were still relatively new, so I went over to a friend's place and typed up these super bootleg signs. CANDY FOR SALE the signs said in huge font. Then I put my home phone number at the bottom so interested buyers could call me and arrange the drop-off like some kind of shady drug deal. I printed them out and walked up and down the streets of our neighborhood, stapling them to telephone poles.

Then I hoisted my big garbage bag over my shoulder like a suburban hobo and knocked on a few doors. It was my first time as a door-to-door salesman, but I figured I might as well leverage the power of some face-to-face interactions with my potential customers.

Keep in mind this was two days after Halloween. Everyone had *so much candy*. Our neighbors humored me, but I'm sure after they shut the door they said to each other, "What are his parents thinking letting this kid go door-to-door selling candy out of a Hefty garbage bag?"

But that wasn't even the worst of it. Within a day of my posting the flyers around the neighborhood, the police called my parents.

"You know it's against regulations to sell loose candy without a permit," they told my mom.

"Officer, you do know my son is eight years old."

"Well, ma'am, your son still needs to go take those signs down."

Apparently, I was violating all sorts of laws trying to sell and distribute food without a license. Of course, my mom had *not* given "sell the candy" as an option on her drop-down menu. Luckily for me, my parents were more amused than angry, and they went with me to take down all the neighborhood signs.

My dad talks about how that was my first encounter with the regulatory limitations in conducting business, but it certainly wouldn't be the last.

Why share this story with you? Because it illuminates a few themes that form the backbone of this book:

1.   There is a massive problem with how we eat as modern Americans. The fact that we have a national Celebrate Candy Day (Halloween) is emblematic of how processed food has overtaken rational, healthy, and less sugar-infused nutrition for everyone, but especially kids. We have become disconnected from our kitchens and our food, and we are suffering as a consequence.

2. Building a food business—*any food business*—is incredibly difficult. I experienced my first run-in with the regulators at a young age. Building a food business that enables transparency, convenience, sustainability, high quality, and value has historically been nearly impossible. We started Plated to use technology to reconnect people to their food and the experience of preparing and sharing it. A new breed of food companies like Plated is required if we are going to feed ten billion people fresh, real food by 2050. We fervently believe that feeding our planet fresh, real food requires bold imagination and tech-centric innovation.

3. Life is complicated. Eating doesn't need to be. Integrating cooking into our eating routine can make us happier, healthier, and more connected to the people and world around us.

From Tragedy to Taking the Entrepreneurial Plunge

I had a sunny childhood like any happy kid in the suburbs—until the event that changed everything. When I was fourteen years old, our family experienced a crisis that profoundly altered the course of my life and would forever shape the way I saw the world.

Life Can Disappear in a Flash

We had known the Merollas forever. At least that's how it felt. They lived down the street from us, and their three kids lined up pretty

close to my siblings and me in age. We first met the Merollas because
their mom, Susan, was my dad's marathon partner. Even in the
scorching summer months, my dad and Susan spent a dozen hours
a week in training. It paid off; they both successfully ran the New
York City Marathon in November 1992.

Just a few weeks later, in December of the same year, Susan was
diagnosed with breast cancer. The doctors caught it very early, and
everyone was hopeful they'd be able to treat it with radiation and
chemotherapy.

Susan was the first person I knew with cancer. She often came
over to our house, bringing the boys to play with my brother and
me. I remember the wigs and outrageous hats she wore after all her
hair fell out. As a kid, it was scary to see changes like that happening, but she always handled everything with grace and humor. She
was one tough lady.

Susan fought a long, hard battle against breast cancer, but in
1996, four years after her diagnosis, the cancer won. We were as
prepared for Susan's death as you can be, but when she finally lost
her fight, we were all devastated. Our families stuck together like
magnets. We were raised Jewish, and they were raised Catholic, but
that didn't matter. We spent most holidays and school vacations together. My parents even arranged for the boys to be in the same
class at school and on the same soccer team.

The week before Labor Day in 1998, my family spent ten days
at the beach on Long Island with the Merollas. It was the tail end of
summer, the last big hurrah before the school year, and we had a
great time. We went Jet-Skiing and ate mozzarella sticks at a crummy
diner. After the holiday week, we all returned, sluggish and sun-
burned, reluctantly ready for the new school year. I was moving to
a new school for ninth grade, and my mind was occupied with
thoughts of what high school girls looked like.

The call came on a sunny Saturday morning. My mom answered
the phone. It was one of the Merolla boys, and he was scared. My

mom rushed out of the house immediately, still in her bathrobe, and sprinted over to the Merollas'. Because she's a doctor, she immediately understood Joe was dying.

By the time the ambulance got there, he was gone.

The only relatives the Merollas had were family in Massachusetts and an older grandmother in Brooklyn, and for the kids to move to either place would have caused major tumult. They would have had to change schools and move to a completely new community, and they had already been through so much.

Instead, my parents just looked at each other and then looked at the kids and said, "You'll come live with us."

Within a matter of days, my parents worked with an extraordinary lawyer to make everything happen, becoming the official guardians. The members of the Merollas' extended family were incredibly supportive; they knew the kids were already very close to our family and that in some ways, blending the two families together was the most natural thing in the world.

Two weeks later, all three Merolla kids moved into our house, and overnight we went from being a family of six to a family of nine. We had become a modern-day *Brady Bunch*.

Within a few weeks, it felt like the Merollas had always been there. We looked kind of similar, and we really did act like brothers and sisters. I went from having three to six siblings in an instant; the only difference was that half of them were biologically related to me and the other half weren't. We'd go on family vacations to Arizona to visit my grandparents, and when we'd roll into the hotel, everybody would stare at our huge family—seven noisy kids, ranging in age from five to sixteen. Sometimes we'd do weird stuff like grab each other's butts just to screw with people. We deployed a potent combination of humor and love to overcome the tragedy and transition that deeply affected all nine of us.

Humor can be a very powerful tool for building culture and camaraderie, especially when times are tough.

Make Family Meals a Mandate

Meanwhile, my mom put her career on hold for four years so she could be a stay-at-home mom, caring for the kids and holding the family together. Both my parents did everything in their power to make sure life went on normally—at least as normal as life would ever be after tragedy. We had exploded from six to nine overnight, and that brought with it a whole new set of changes and challenges. My parents understood that we needed to gather together, and one place we did that was the same place families had been gathering together for millennia: the kitchen table.

Meals were an extremely important part of our lives. Sitting down at the table, eating well, eating together—these were the staples of our family, and they were nonnegotiable. Never was that truer than when we'd gather around the table for Shabbat dinner, the special meals Jewish families have on Friday nights.

My siblings and I were raised Jewish, but we weren't *that* observant. We were the sort of Jews who'd go to temple on the high holidays. But every Friday night we would say prayers at home and light candles for Shabbat. My mom would serve roasted chicken and challah, delicious braided bread, and we'd say a blessing over the candles, bread, and wine. We'd also pass around a tzedakah, or charity box, and each of us would put in a couple of coins. It was more symbolic than anything, a way to give back to those who were less fortunate.

For as long as I can remember, Shabbat was a mandate in our family. Even in high school when we were dying to go out with our friends on the weekends, my mom expected us to be home for dinner Friday night. We were all scattered in every which direction, but we'd still come together once a week no matter what else was going on in all our lives. It's been a special thing in our family for as long as I can remember. Even once we all started going off to college, the rule was that if you were in town, you had to be butt in chair.

For my mom, it was important that food be about more than just nutrition and physical sustenance. When I was a kid, a lot of data came out about how kids from families who have meals together every night grow up to be happier and more successful later in life. As a pediatrician, my mom was very attuned to this data, and after the Merolla kids moved in with us, it became all the more important to give all seven of her kids a strong foundation from which to build.

Family meals had always been special, but from that point on, they became an extremely important part of our lives.

My mom wanted us to love food, love shopping for fresh ingredients, cooking, and eating together. The way she saw it, our big home-cooked meals were the glue holding the family together. And it was a *lot* of glue. Seven growing children meant seven hungry mouths to feed. She cooked three full chickens every Friday afternoon for Shabbat.

Keep in mind that a couple of years later, my mom had *four teenage boys* in the house at the same time. We were all superactive, involved in different kinds of sports and after-school activities, so we were ravenous. We would stuff our faces every morning before school and then get home at night and devour anything we could find in the house. My dad did a ton of grilling on the weekends— we all loved a good steak. It probably would have saved money in the long run if my parents had just invested in their own herd of cattle.

We had a commercial freezer in the basement, the kind you see at a restaurant where the lid opens on top, and we had mountains of things stocked in there. The house was a central hub; it was filled with kids constantly. It was packed with boisterous activity and people eating anything and everything they could find. Oftentimes we had at least ten people for dinner—seven kids, two parents, and the inevitable friend one of us invited over, or a friend who still hadn't been picked up from practice. "Once you're at ten, what's one or two more?" my dad used to say. He would always come home with a couple of gallons of milk. "You didn't have to call and check," he says.

I'm lucky because my mom was a very good (and creative) cook, and my dad was more than passable himself. He cooked the way his mother in Istanbul had cooked before him—a pinch of this, a bit of that, hardly ever referring to a cookbook. As a family, we didn't just grab food and then run out the door to do something else. My dad always made sure napkins and silverware were set for every meal. Eating was worth stopping and sitting down for. It wasn't just an activity—it was a central activity that served as a centerpiece of family life.

But I'll be honest: My brothers and sisters spent far more time in the kitchen than I did, slicing and dicing, having conversations with my mom while doing food prep. You know how there are some kids who wander over to the stove when their mom or dad is cooking and say, "Gee, what's that yellow stuff? Is that saffron?" I was not that kid. (I understand it's kind of ironic given what I do today. In our office, I now wander over and ask questions and steal bites of deliciousness and get yelled at by our culinary team for ruining our photo shoots.)

I was excellent at eating food, but I wasn't particularly interested in learning how to prepare it. In high school, I was more interested in other things, like girls and getting in trouble—preferably at the same time.

Toward the end of high school, the low-carb diet craze started. I had an obese buddy who used Atkins as an excuse to eat nothing but bacon for an entire month. He ended up breaking out in horrendous acne and reverted to his standard foot-long meatball Parmesan sub. I was a big dude—six foot two and two hundred pounds by the time I was a high school freshman—and I was briefly swept up in the Atkins craze myself. I spent a few weeks subsisting on cans of tuna with a glob of spicy mustard on top. My strict tuna diet helped me shred my tummy—in addition to hours in the gym every day—but I perpetually smelled like tuna. It was pretty gross.

I threw myself at Atkins the same way I threw myself at anything. After watching what had happened to my friends' parents, I lived every minute like it was my last. My awareness of life's one-way march led me to push myself to live and experience life at warp speed. If I was only here for a very finite chunk of time, I had to cram everything possible into my living days and nights. After high school, I charged full-force into the future. Big challenges, big missions, and moving fast would come to define my life.

Mountain Man

In college, I found that I was like a shark—as long as I constantly kept moving forward, I survived. Laps around the pond outside my dorm turned into running thirty, then forty, then fifty or more miles at a time. I'd stuff my backpack full of Clif Bars, PowerGels, cookies, and whatever else I could get my hands on and jump onto my motorcycle. Then I'd drive up from Hanover on the Vermont border straight into the White Mountains in New Hampshire, where I would run for six, eight, ten, sometimes even fifteen hours at a time. I was a total wild man. Alone in the mountains for hours on end, I wouldn't even pack water—I'd just drink out of streams whenever I could find them. I'd always hated being the chubby, big kid, and now, for the first time in my life, I could eat whatever I wanted. I'd scarf down thousands of calories over the course of a day running forty, fifty, and eventually over eighty miles at a time through the mountains.

Part of what drew me to running those crazy distances was that I could stuff my face and burn it all off. My running allowed me to unleash my inner fat kid, the one who wished he could have eaten that whole Hefty bag of Halloween candy. I felt like I had found the loophole, a way to eat whatever I wanted while also feeling incredibly alive. In retrospect, I realize that I was literally and figuratively trying to outrun both my adolescent inner demons and my bad eating habits.

In the long term, it's impossible to outrun an unhealthy relationship with food.

Going to Extremes to Find Myself

I was going to be the youngest person to ski to the North Pole. It was a totally wacky scheme I'd cooked up, the kind people have at 3:00 A.M. when they can't sleep, and then the next morning, in the cold light of day, they realize it was totally nuts. But for me, the cold light of day did not have a sobering effect.

If people aren't making fun of your dreams, your dreams might not be big enough.

I spent spring break my sophomore year in the Canadian Arctic doing a ten-day polar-exploration training session to prepare myself for my expedition. I found a retired polar explorer named Paul Landry who agreed to teach me the basics: polar bear protection, how to pack and pull a sled over ice, how to cook and camp when it's negative forty degrees. I drove up from Dartmouth to Montreal, slept in my car, and then flew four hours north to get to Iqaluit, the capital city of Nunavut. Nunavut is the biggest territory in Canada, the size of all of Western Europe combined—and most people have never even heard of it.

And here I was—in the middle of Iqaluit, this frigid little city with a population of fewer than seven thousand people. The whole city is under ice nine months of the year, and when I got there in March, the temperature had not risen above zero in six months.

There's not much in town, and all the buildings are specially constructed to withstand high winds and ultracold temperatures. There's one supermarket and one McDonald's, both tucked into special buildings because of the extreme cold.

There wasn't a lot going on in Iqaluit, but there was one little pub. They stopped serving beer after 8:00 P.M. since they didn't want people coming in and getting drunk and dying outside in the cold. But on my first day in the city, Paul took me to the pub and we had beer and a dish called muktuk—whale blubber stew.

If you think eating whale blubber means eating fat, you are correct. It was flaccid and rubbery. Not much taste. Imagine chewing on a tire made out of balloons and flavorless salmon skin. It was definitely not delicious. But the Inuit had to eat fatty, tasteless provisions like muktuk in order to survive because it was so freaking cold.

"Because we are essentially living inside of a freezer, our bodies are burning an insane number of calories just to stay warm," Paul explained to me. "The more you can eat, the better your chances of survival."

It was basically "muktuk or freeze to death." I chose muktuk.

I spent the rest of my time out on the ice. I camped next to Paul's sled dogs and fell asleep to the Arctic Ocean creaking and cracking beneath my head.

Toward the end of the camp, Paul spent a day teaching me how to cross open stretches of water. The best time of year to make a bid from Canada to the North Pole is the spring, when at night it's negative forty instead of negative one hundred. The downside is that the ice starts to melt, and you have to cross open stretches of slushy black water.

Paul showed me the technique, which involved a graceful balancing from ice blob to ice blob. When it was my turn, I took three steps, slipped, and fell into the Arctic Ocean up to my neck. It was negative twenty-five degrees outside.

Paul acted quickly. He pulled me out of the ocean, and as I felt the water begin to crystallize all over my body, he had me roll on the ice, strip off all my clothes, and run in circles to stay warm while he threw a tent up and fired on the stove. I spent the rest of the day thawing out in the tent, feeling enormously lucky things had turned out okay. After that harrowing incident, I realized that I wanted my life to be about more than freezing to death alone at the North Pole.

I decided that skiing to the North Pole was my version of proving myself to the world, but I wasn't even remotely sure what I was trying to prove. I wanted to have an impact on the world. I wanted to be a part of something bigger than myself and improve people's lives.

My time training in the Arctic taught me that you don't need millions of dollars or years of instruction to turn your dreams into reality—you just need the right dream and enough passion to pressure test it against reality.

To Make Impact, Make Profit

After I graduated from Dartmouth in 2006, the U.S. government paid for me to move to East Java, Indonesia. I lived in Madiun, a small city where my home base was a local teacher's house. From my front porch, I had views of the sun setting over a rice paddy with a dormant volcano on the horizon. I paid fifty dollars per month for three meals per day, house cleaning, and all the locally harvested and roasted Javanese coffee I could stomach. I was thrown into a totally foreign culture where the sounds, flavors, and traditions were a daily exercise in adaptation.

In theory, I was there to teach English part-time at a local school. In practice, between Ramadan and a seemingly endless supply of other holidays, I ended up teaching only a few hours per week. With my spare time, I teamed up with a group of local community organizers, and we started a microfinance nonprofit together. The guys that I worked with already had nonprofit status, and we folded our microfinance institution into their organization, Konsorsium Monitoring dan Pemberdayaan Institusi Publik (KOMPIP). These guys were hard-core Democracy rights advocates, and they had weathered the overthrow of the Suharto regime in the late 1990s. When I first met Akbar, the head of KOMPIP, he invited me into his one-room, tin-roof home that he shared with his wife and young son. We shared a meal of red rice, sautéed vegetables, fried tempeh, and a spicy Javanese peanut sauce called *pecel*. Sushi and Chinese takeout had been the extent of my Asian food education growing up, and the textures, spices, and flavors in Java expanded my mental horizons of what was possible for food. We slept on the cement floor on top of rattan mats and shared steaming cups of local coffee in the morning. They were fascinated with this big, goofy, white American guy, and they were excited to put my microfinance theories into practice.

I had done research on microfinance as part of my honors thesis. The basic concept was giving small loans (under a hundred dollars in most cases) to people who otherwise couldn't access loans from banks or credit cards. Most of the loans were used by laborers to buy brick-making machines or by farmers to buy seeds or tools for their plots. In place of using traditional collateral (like a house or car), we used the relationships within the community. We found that our clients would beg, borrow, and steal before committing the cultural faux pas of failing to repay a loan.

Over the course of the next year, I learned how a small, agile, creative kind of enterprise could make a big difference where large, more established organizations were unable or unwilling to meet consumer demand.

Overall, I saw how small efforts on a small scale could make a difference in individuals' lives. Following an earthquake in the area, one of our clients broke her leg. The bone broke through the skin, and with no insurance or savings to pay for a hospital visit, weeks later, the area between her knee and ankle was festering and gruesome. Through KOMPIP, she was able to take out a loan, pay for surgery, and return to work in a few months. Otherwise, she most likely would have been crippled for life and indefinitely dependent on the goodwill of her neighbors.

I had some exciting adventures while I was living in Indonesia, traveling to the outer islands like Mentawai, Sumba, and Lombok. Microfinance was exciting, too—or at least it had the potential to be.

The Merollas' grandma Margie died around this time, and in her will, she left me $5,000. I put that money into the KOMPIP microfinance portfolio. We ultimately raised hundreds of thousands of additional dollars from folks ranging from the regional government to the Ford Foundation to Coca-Cola. But no matter how much money we raised from donors, it felt like we were always behind the ball. I was spending all my time writing grant proposals and none of my time in the field interacting with clients, working to solve their problems.

This ended up being a big lesson for me: It is incredibly hard and time-consuming to constantly rely on donors to fund your organization.

We were disbursing hundreds of loans, but there were millions of people who needed our help. Even if I stayed in Java for my entire life, at this rate, we would only impact a small percentage of the population. I realized I needed to be more disciplined and rigorous in evaluating how I could be most helpful and where I wanted to spend my time.

Who should I work with to accomplish as much as possible? What safeguards could I put in place to protect my valuable time and resources?

That was when I first discovered the concept of the force multiplier: You as an individual can only do so much, but if you can inspire others to action, you can accomplish infinitely more.

Even in the jungle, I was learning invaluable lessons that would serve me well later on as a marine, entrepreneur, and business owner.

I tried to convince the KOMPIP guys to pivot our model from not-for-profit to profit-seeking, but they were adamantly opposed. These guys had seen how money had corrupted their country, leading to a cash- and military-fueled regime, and they wanted nothing to do with it. I could feel my time in Java coming to an end, and a few months later, I returned to the United States for graduate school. I understood nonprofits served a very important role in the world, but I also realized that I wanted to have the force multiplier impact of building my team around turning a profit.

I wanted to build a mission-driven organization in a sustainable and scalable way that was not limited by donor funding.

I knew I needed harder analysis skills and a better-informed toolbox for looking at the world. This led me to Harvard for graduate school.

"Networking"

At Harvard Business School (HBS), I watched my classmates job hunt and land huge bonuses and sign six-figure contracts at private equity firms and hedge funds. That life held no appeal for me. I knew that someday I wanted to start my own mission-driven business, combining the best of what I learned in Java and at HBS. But first I felt compelled to become a leader, to serve my country, and to live a life of high adventure. I wanted to be a marine.

But I had also met Nimmi while in business school. I was in the gym with a buddy when I first saw her, and I immediately knew she was special. My friend and I spent the remainder of our workout trying to set up a nonawkward introduction, which went about as well as it sounds. Nimmi was also doing her MBA, but she was a year ahead.

For some reason, she gave me a chance, and the more I got to know her, the more I got to like her. She was tall and beautiful and regularly had gaggles of friends in stitches with her irreverent sense of humor. She could also cook a mean omelet. Her parents were immigrants from South India, and she had grown up the town over from where my mom grew up in Minnesota. When she first met my grandma, they spent a solid half hour sharing their recipes for Marshmallow Fluff salad, some midwestern delicacy that I still to this day can't wrap my head around. She was the kind of girl you'd ski to the North Pole for, and I felt compelled to pursue a traditional career path to make her happy and prove that I was serious about our relationship and that I could provide for her.

A few weeks after graduating from Harvard Business School, I became an active-duty Marine Corps officer—the first person since World War II to join the Marines *after* going to HBS. In an effort to convince Nimmi that I was not just some adrenaline junkie, I also accepted and deferred an offer from Goldman Sachs. Before reporting for my year of active-duty training with the Marines, Nimmi and I traveled to Cambodia, where I asked her to marry me. It was almost one hundred degrees, humidity so thick you could cut it, and after carrying the ring around in rolled-up socks for a week, I totally surprised her. She said yes!

We spent the rest of our trip chilling out, sampling various forms of Cambodian cuisine, which ranged from the unusual (grilled snake and fried crickets) to phenomenal (lok lak beef stir fry). We flew out of Phnom Penh, where the omnipresent sight of beggars missing limbs was a reminder of what the Khmer Rouge or any other totalitarian regime can do to humanity. Again, I found meaning in my decision to join the military. A few days later, I reported for active duty with the Marine Corps.

Picture of an Evolved Eater

Alyssa Wand, New York, New York

Alyssa is a mother of two boys (three and six years old) and is a self-proclaimed foodie. She has been a Plated customer for almost four years. She lives with her husband in the Tribeca neighborhood of New York City.

Alyssa says, "I am very particular about what I feed my family. And we're very health conscious. I don't do a lot of processed foods, no canned goods, only wild-caught fish, and always 100 percent grass-fed organic beef. I really don't do any packaged food for my children. So I'm like the mean mom that doesn't allow Goldfish."

Alyssa enjoys cooking, so before Plated, dinner was good—it just wasn't great. Getting the recipe, then shopping, then making sure she had all the right portions of all the ingredients—doing all of this was too difficult to ensure that dinner was regularly living up to Alyssa's expectations.

She adds, "I got into this habit probably like a year ago where I was cooking two dinners every night. I would cook something for the kids that was a little simpler. I would feed them and then put them to bed. And only then would I start cooking for my husband and me. And I literally did that for a year. And eventually I was like, 'I'm going to go crazy! I have to cook and clean up two meals a night! What is this, a restaurant?' I just couldn't do it anymore!"

Alyssa then discovered the Plated three-portion offering. Now she only cooks one meal per night, and the whole family eats Plated.

Alyssa concludes, "I feel like it's expanding my kids' palates, because I'm not cooking mac and cheese and chicken fingers. And my older son has become a really good eater. My kids are growing up eating mostly Plated meals for dinner! I mean, I'm a huge advocate. It's been great. It's made my life a lot easier, my family appreciates it, and it allows me to expand our repertoire and palate of foods we're eating without slaving away in the kitchen.

"I depend on you guys. You allow me to feed my family the way they deserve to be fed."

First Course

The Story of Humans and Food:
How We Got to This Place Where Food Is a Problem
Instead of a Solution

1

Our Food Is Killing Us

It was the summer of 2011. The last part of my Marine Corps training consisted of a multiweek mission in the Mojave Desert. We were stationed aboard Marine Corps Air Ground Combat Center Twentynine Palms, a 932-square-mile sprawling expanse of desert and mountains nearly the size of Rhode Island. The base is so big that several years ago, a marine got lost in training during a night exercise. He wandered off into the desert, following lights on the horizon. His skeleton was found four months later.

The Mojave was fierce and unrelenting. Home to cacti, rugged snowcapped mountains, North America's most venomous rattle-snake, and twenty-three thousand tons of dropped explosives per year, Twentynine Palms was about as far removed from the rest of America as you could get while being in the continental United States.

Our company of Marines spent most of our time at Twentynine Palms awake, moving, and trying to convince our instructors that we were thriving. But surviving, let alone thriving, was not easy. We went days on end without sleeping. Temperatures in the midday sun reached over 120 degrees. We hiked over broken ridgelines, carrying hundreds of pounds of ammunition, weapons, communication gear, and water. No matter how much water I drank, I was constantly suffering from dehydration headaches. And the "food." Let me tell you about the food.

This won't come as a surprise to you if you've spent any time in the military—or in a zombie apocalypse—but military-grade MREs are probably the worst food humanity has ever invented. Worse than Spam. Worse than a Hefty garbage bag filled with candy. Worse than the flaccid undercooked mystery meat you find in a Cincinnati airport lounge. And potentially even worse than a Kit-Kat lasagna.

We didn't eat fresh food for weeks. Instead, we tore into MREs anytime we had five minutes to scarf down calories. Sometimes, when I was feeling masochistic, I'd look at the ingredient list on the back of the desert-drab package. The recipe title for menu 16 was "Rib Shaped Barbecue Flavor Pork Patty." I could run a whole seminar breaking down those six words. What the hell is "rib shaped"? What word is "barbecue flavor" modifying, or is it its own food group? And pray tell, what the *F* is a "pork patty"?

Once I'd torn into the main package, the smaller cardboard boxes inside were covered with the names of dire-sounding chemicals and preservatives that you would never find in a standard American kitchen. Dextrose, sodium tripolyphosphate, sodium diacetate, corn syrup solids, cellulose gum, malic acid, smoke flavor, maltodextrin, partially hydrogenated cottonseed oil, modified corn starch, tricalcium phosphate, and my favorite, flavorings. Some of that stuff was harmless, as I learned from a quick Google search, ingredients you'd find in the baking powder sitting innocuously in your pantry. But I couldn't even figure out what half those words *were*, let alone pronounce them. And there I was, eating nothing but these strange-sounding concoctions every day, because like my mom always said, "Hunger is the world's greatest chef."

Food was at the forefront of my mind, more than it had ever been before. We were out in the middle of the desert, sweating and bleeding and learning how to hump gear and shoot guns to serve our country. And what were they feeding us? Consumable Riskily Altered Provisions—CRAP. I understood why, too. Most MREs have to be highly processed so that the food survives the extended shelf life of active duty. You can't exactly eat a warm spinach salad with herbed goat cheese and heirloom pears when you're out fighting guys in Afghanistan.

But what happens when the troops come home? The real problem is that it isn't just marines and soldiers on active duty eating riskily altered foods. It's millions of Americans—civilians living out their daily lives, many not even aware that the food they eat is killing them. I started rooting around for some hard statistics, and what I found shocked me. During the whole war on terror, 6,717 American servicemen and servicewomen died in combat or due to terrorist attacks. Meanwhile, in 2013 alone: *611,105 Americans died from heart disease; 584,881 died from cancer; 75,578 died from diabetes.*[1] According to a study in the *American Journal of Public Health*, obesity is associated with *nearly one in five U.S. deaths.*[2] That's one in five of your friends, family, and colleagues, dying every year from preventable causes—most of which are related to our riskily altered American diet.

As pediatrician Dr. Harvey Karp said in the documentary *Fed Up*, "If a foreign nation was causing our children to become obese—that's going to affect their health and hurt their happiness, cause them to be depressed, have poor self-esteem—if a foreign nation were doing that to our children, we'd probably go to war."[3]

During my time in the desert, I thought a lot about what it meant to eat riskily altered provisions versus real food. After a long mission, let alone a yearlong deployment, marines talked of "the golden loaf"—this referred to both the trans fat–infused corn bread snacks in MREs and the appearance of a bowel movement

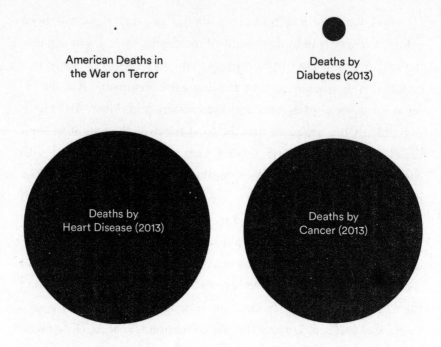

American Deaths in
the War on Terror

Deaths by
Diabetes (2013)

Deaths by
Heart Disease (2013)

Deaths by
Cancer (2013)

after exclusively eating the snacks for weeks on end. Neither was pleasant or natural.

How had my eating choices affected my health and happiness in ways I had never admitted to myself or anyone else? I knew well enough the kind of riskily altered stuff my friends and I ate back in New York even when we *weren't* in the middle of the desert with limited options for keeping food fresh and edible.

After finishing my active duty and returning to New York to work on Wall Street, I was still a long way off from being an Evolved Eater. One night, I tried to cook for my wife, Nimmi, and nearly burned the house down. I had pawed through a truly terrifying number of processed foods in our own pantry. Why wasn't I eating good food? Why wasn't I *cooking* good food?

If America had a disease when it came to eating, I had it, too. I was hooked on a FAD—the Flawed American Diet. I needed a palate cleanser. The question was, where to begin?

Why Our Food Is Killing Us

The United States is called a melting pot for a reason. As a relatively young country stewed together from the raw ingredients of many different immigrant traditions, each with its own depth of food culture, America has never had a unifying culinary tradition to guide us. My dad is a Turkish Jew who grew up eating hummus, baba ghanoush, and baklava in Istanbul. My mom's family is of German stock—they've farmed their own homestead in South Dakota since the 1880s, and my grandma kept warm potatoes in her pockets when she walked to school across the frozen prairie (we'll hear a lot more about this in chapter 4 when I pay a visit to the ol' family farm). I married an Indian gal whose parents emigrated from Andhra Pradesh and Tamil Nadu, where they grew up eating dosa, idli sambar, and veda.

My story is far from unique. Most Americans boast equally diverse legacies, hailing from a long line of rich cultural traditions. But while our culinary tradition affords us a tantalizing mélange of tastes, the lack of a consistent food culture has left us vulnerable to the modern-day food marketer.

After being yelled at through TV ads, magazine spreads, and celebrity endorsements for the vast majority of our lives, how can we not be both schizophrenic and confused about how to even define what "good food" means? I sure didn't know how to define it. Add to this every new diet fad—many of which are championed by a *New York Times* bestselling book, and several of which I've tried—and our bewilderment is justified.

Why is it so hard to find the truth? Why is there so much confusion and conflicting advice? These were the questions I started to ask myself. I wanted cold facts and hard data on what to eat, how much of it, and why—and I couldn't find anything conclusive. This baffled me. I needed to take a different approach.

I went to my buddy Lance Martin, who had just received his Ph.D. in applied physics and bioengineering at Stanford. Lance lives and breathes this sort of stuff—big data, analytics—and I wanted to get his take on nutrition science. I knew he would have a well-formed opinion on the matter—and he did.

Lance had taken Peter Thiel's start-up class at Stanford. Peter Thiel is the billionaire cofounder of PayPal. He was the first outside investor in Facebook, and he has invested in and cofounded multiple other billion-dollar businesses. It is not outrageous to claim that he is one of the best venture capitalists in history.

Lance told me about Peter's talk about "secrets"—things that other people aren't thinking about that might have big potential for a start-up. To paraphrase Peter: Most top scientists have gone into fields other than nutrition over the past couple of decades. There's not really an incentive to study nutrition today, and nutrition science has been chronically underfunded. And now we have an obesity explosion. As Lance says, "Getting nutrition right isn't quite low-hanging fruit, but there are reasons to think that the right people haven't been incentivized to look at it hard enough." Or more insidiously, that the wrong people have been incentivized to look the other way in the face of data that would otherwise help us solve our nutrition problems.

"I think Peter's right," Lance said. "Having done a Ph.D. at Stanford, I've spent the last few years around a bunch of top scientists. There is plenty of interest in health data—molecular mechanisms, cancer, disease models, those sorts of issues. But very few people are really looking at wellness and nutrition. I have come across very few top research programs that offer a program in nutrition. The top scientific journals are rarely, if ever, publishing articles on it, and almost no one is funding these kinds of studies."

Why not? The answer to this question involves a much more nuanced answer that we'll unpack in chapter 7. Lance has one of the best minds of anyone I know. He completed Peter Thiel's class, where he was advised to pursue a "secret" no one was investigating—namely, nutrition. But did he jump into a research project or launch a start-up around the idea? Nope. Lance works on the data science team at Uber.

Knowing that certainly didn't help me, an average guy who just wanted to feel healthier, look better, and enjoy my food instead of constantly stressing about it. My own body was sending me confusing messages. I wanted to look good. I was a fitness junkie—I never wanted to go back to being the chubby kid who gets poked in the tummy at the pool, but I also wanted to stuff my face with greasy, sugary, delicious nomnoms, especially after a few drinks. I was finally becoming aware of the glaring disconnect between how we eat and who we aim to be—but I still didn't have a clue what to do about it. And that is true for most Americans.

We crave movie-star abs, but we choose processed carbs and sugary drinks over leafy greens. We want to feel and look great, so we hit the studio that offers the latest fitness craze after work—and then grab a greasy slice of pizza to sate our appetite after one drink at the bar. Guilty as charged; I've done all these things.

Here in America, we have irrational expectations about eating. We have irrational expectations about a lot of things, actually, but eating is the one thing we all do every single day. Food is, in so many ways, at the heart of our lives—and when we fail at food, we fail miserably.

As I returned to New York fresh out of the Marine Corps to start my new corporate job, I felt weighed down by reality. Tens of millions of Americans were struggling with obesity, shoveling in riskily altered provisions every day, and suffering significant consequences. But what if we took control over this and understood we had the power to change our circumstances? Or even if we were already eating okay, how could we make it easy to eat great?

In America, stories of food failure are quickly becoming the "new normal." More than one-third of U.S. adults are obese: a whopping

34.9 percent, or 78.6 million people.[4] We pay a premium for obesity: The estimated annual medical cost of obesity in our country is over $190 billion—*nearly 21 percent* of annual medical spending in the United States.[5]

But the real cost is not financial; it's about losing the people we love. Reams of research linking obesity to poor health has been done over the last few decades, and the verdict is in: Obesity leads to heart disease, stroke, and type 2 diabetes—three leading causes of preventable death.

Emphasis here on *preventable*. But in order to prevent something from happening, you have to know how it happens in the first place. As an incoming high school freshman, I was six foot two and two hundred pounds. You know that awkward big kid lumbering through the halls of your high school who didn't know what to do with his hands and feet? That was me. I played basketball and lacrosse, but the football coaches were always trying to recruit me. My mom was scared I'd get a concussion and wouldn't let me play—she has always been ahead of the curve.

I was made fun of in elementary and middle school because of my weight. I weighed the same in seventh grade as I did in twelfth, but once my height shot up and I leaned out, the teasing stopped. But this seminal time of being chubby and the center of many fat jokes had a profound impact on me. Even today as a thirty-two-year-old who can deadlift five hundred pounds and run three miles in under eighteen minutes with single-digit body fat, I still harbor an internal echo of my adolescent overweight self.

For the more than seventy-eight million obese Americans—and the inflammation, the arthritis, the high blood pressure, the diabetes that comes with obesity—feeling crummy is a given. When you're heavy, it's hard to exercise, which fosters a vicious cycle. *The Lancet*, one of the world's most prestigious medical journals, recently reported that physical inactivity has now surpassed smoking as a leading cause of death. The study estimates that 6 percent of heart disease, 7 percent of type 2 diabetes, and 10 percent of colon and breast cancers are linked to a lack of activity.[6]

Always interested in human psychology, I started thinking about food in terms of Maslow's hierarchy of needs. Abraham Maslow was a psychologist who studied positive human qualities and the lives of world-class humans. In 1954, Maslow created the hierarchy of needs and expressed his theories in his book *Motivation and Personality*. As you can see in the rendering below, ahead of even safety and security, food forms the base of the pyramid. Food is the most fundamental need we have as humans.

If you don't figure out food, hardly anything else matters—not family, friends, self-esteem, confidence, creativity, or self-actualization. That's because without a strong food foundation, it is impossible to experience the emotions, ambitions, and relationships that make life worth living.

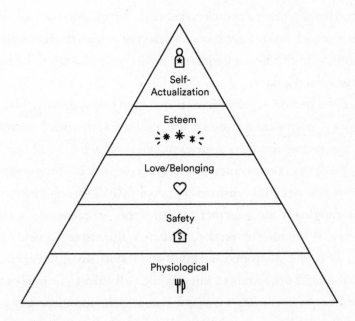

You Get What You Pay For

The fast-food phenomenon is a major culprit in perpetuating the FAD. As modern-day Americans, we want everything in our lives to be fast, from our transportation to our Wi-Fi connections. Unfortunately, this preference has spilled over into our food.

Fast food is all about supersized portions and low prices. Like so much else in life, with food, you truly get what you pay for. Fast food chains are able to sell hamburgers for under a dollar by stripping out quality. And low-quality food literally kills us. There's ample evidence that frequent fast-food consumption contributes to overeating and weight gain. One study followed three thousand young adults for a period of thirteen years, ultimately finding that those who had higher fast-food-intake levels at the beginning weighed an average of *thirteen pounds more* than their non-fast-food-eating counterparts by the end.[7]

There are so many problems and there is so much work to be done that it's easy to get overwhelmed. But unlike many of my predecessors who wrote great books that condemned the industrial food complex, in this book, and in my life in general, I try to be both an optimist and a doer.

Let's be honest—we have come a long way already. Many elements of our twenty-first-century food world are much better than they were twenty, fifteen, or even five years ago.

Food has taken center stage. The celebrity chef movement has brought cooking into millions of people's lives through various avenues ranging from "gourmet airplane food" to network TV competitions. What appears on the menu in Williamsburg quickly makes its way to the gastropub in Dallas and eventually influences everyday food culture. And cooking, while still hard to fit into our hurried lives, is becoming viewed less as a chore and more as a joy. As chef Dan Barber writes, "After Wolfgang Puck reimagined pizza in

the 1980s at his fine-dining restaurant Spago, in Los Angeles—
smoked salmon instead of tomatoes; crème fraîche instead of
cheese—gourmet pizza spread to every corner of America, eventually culminating in the supermarket frozen food aisle. We now have
the power to quickly popularize certain products and ingredients—
in some cases, as with certain fish, to the point of commercial
extinction—and increasingly we do, with dizzying speed and effect. But we also possess the potential to get people to rethink their
eating habits."[8]

Activist chefs like Dan Barber have helped highlight the perils
of the Flawed American Diet. They have exposed the connections
between how we eat and our heavy environmental, social, and health
footprint. The poet, farmer, and environmental activist Wendell
Berry wrote that we understand that eating "is inescapably an agricultural act, and that how we eat determines, to a considerable extent, how the world is used."[9]

Folks like Michael Pollan, Mark Bittman, Gary Taubes, Marion
Nestle, and Dan Barber have helped to elevate the American food
conversation. "Farm to table" has become so widely known and
popular that it is satirized to the point of absurdity, where chickens
have names and wear clothes.

> Americans have more "non-conventional" food options than
> ever before (farmers' markets, organic food, farm-to-table
> restaurants) and more information about how to cook (TV and
> app-based cooking shows, an infinite number of online recipes).
> In 1994 there were only 1,755 farmers' markets in the United
> States. Today there are over 8,000.[10]

Today food is safer, cheaper, and more convenient than at any
prior point in human history. Through their construction of a processed food–centric supply chain, Big Food has, for better or worse,
largely solved issues of food scarcity and food safety in the United

States and, increasingly, around the world. Let's acknowledge the monumental achievement of being able to grow, process, manufacture, package, store, and distribute enough shelf-stable calories to feed billions of people. This is a massive win for humanity and the twentieth-century efforts to industrialize food and should be recognized as such.

But you won't find executives and directors popping celebratory bottles of champagne in Big Food boardrooms. On the contrary, they have an enormous problem on their hands: Consumers are increasingly looking for and buying alternatives to the riskily altered provisions that Big Food exclusively promoted for so long. Packaged-food sales in the United States are falling at a rate of 1 percent a year, which doesn't seem like very much, until you compare it to the fact that Plated has been achieving a triple-digit growth rate since we started. And we are not alone.

My buddy Irving Fain is a former social media entrepreneur whose next business is Bowery Farming, a network of hydroponic, indoor, vertical farms. His first "farm" is located in a refurbished warehouse fifteen minutes from where I live. His prototype start-up farm is capable of growing more crops on less land with 5 percent of the water consumption of a typical traditional farm. His head of operations spent a decade building automation technology for the car industry in Detroit, and the first person he hired was a computer vision expert in order to use artificial intelligence and machine learning to optimize everything from water consumption to nutrient distribution to crop yield and packaging. Bowery Farming has already received millions of dollars in venture capital from some of the best early-stage investors in the world.

In chapter 4, we will pay a visit to my family's commodity corn farm in South Dakota. We will see the contrast between traditional farming and where the future of farming needs to go if we are going to feed the planet. As Irving says, "One of the things you realize when you dig into traditional agriculture is that there is a tremendous amount of eyeballing and knowledge transfer from generation to generation in families. And that system exists because prior to just a few years ago, there was no way to collect, analyze, or aggregate large amounts of information with regards to farming. Technology is changing that." Fortunately, folks like Irving are already working hard for a brighter, healthier, more sustainable future.

Healthier, fresher, and more delicious food is slowly making its way to more and more retailers and consumers. Annual sales of organic food are increasing by double digits every year. And for the first time, in 2014, sales topped $100 billion for the "specialty food industry"—what many folks might refer to as "hipster kibble." Eighty-two percent of those sales were made in mainstream stores— places like Safeway and Albertsons. The Jerry Garcia–reminiscent products like quinoa and kale chips that used to reside only in the Phish T-shirt–operated co-op or the Birkenstock-bedecked local health food store are increasingly being bought and sold in places where Big Food once had no competition.[11]

This is all fantastic news for humankind, but let's not fool ourselves into thinking that our work as Evolved Eaters is done. We are living through a curious paradox: Though 79 percent of Americans say they enjoy cooking, *two-thirds* of calories are consumed away from home. And calories consumed away from home tend to be of the riskily altered variety.

Why is this the case? The answer to this inconsistency involves a history lesson that starts three million years ago.

2

Eating Evolution, Part 1:
Cooking Made Us Human

EVOLUTION

DEFINITION:

noun

1. *the process by which different kinds of living organisms are thought to have developed and diversified from earlier forms during the history of the earth.*

2. *the gradual development of something, especially from a simple to a more complex form.*

All right, bear with me for a minute. I'm about to jump up on the soapbox:

I believe that evolution is the greatest single force in the universe and that it is awesome. To oversimplify things, as humans, we are all just vehicles for transporting evolution further down the road. Evolution affects the changes of everything from all species to the entire solar system. It is awesome because evolution is the process that leads to improvement and to building a better future. The things, creatures, and rituals that fail to make it to the future are those that don't work because they are at odds with the laws of the universe and they impede evolution. The desire to evolve is humanity's most pervasive driving force, and it's why we're all here today.

Okay, let me get off my soapbox now.

Why start this chapter off with a tirade on something that almost everyone takes for granted? Because wrapping your head around how quickly and dramatically we humans evolved into our current eating and living habits is essential to understanding how food and dinner came to fail us.

Redefining History

Most of us walk around and have a very tightly defined construct of what "history" means. We have work history, which focuses on the task list today, the deliverables due at the end of the quarter, annual reports, the holiday party—at the extreme, perhaps a decade or two of memory and future aspirations. We have national history. Here in the United States, this goes back to 1776. And we have family history, which spans generations and centuries—some folks can chart back their genealogy over a millennium.

But very few of us walk around thinking about history in terms of tens or hundreds of thousands or millions of years. When I was living in Indonesia, I had a buddy who was a Ph.D. in geology. He walked around with a rock hammer. As we scaled volcanoes on Java or explored jungles in Sumatra, he would crack open small boulders and tell me the history of the area—on the scale of millions and billions of years. He completely changed how I thought about myself relative to the world and the universe.

One hundred thousand years ago, *Homo sapiens* (a.k.a. "humans") were just another type of animal slugging it out for survival on the African savannah. Over the following one hundred millennia, we transformed ourselves into the planetary rulers.

This incredible evolutionary tale is the direct consequence of cooking.

Despite their big brains and sharp stone tools, early humans lived for millions of years in constant fear of predators. They rarely hunted large animals and instead subsisted mainly by gathering plants, scooping up insects, stalking small animals, and eating the rotten flesh left behind by other more powerful carnivores.[1]

This is a key to understanding our history, psychology, and evolution to the modern Flawed American Diet. For millions of years, early humans hunted smaller creatures and gathered what they could, all the while being hunted by larger predators. It was only half a million years ago that several species of man began to hunt large game on a regular basis. Humans only rose to the top of the food chain one hundred thousand years ago.

In the grand scheme of evolutionary history, one hundred thousand years is the equivalent of the blink of a mastodon's eye. My rock hammer—wielding buddy in Sumatra scoffs at one hundred millennia as if it were preschool graduation. However, that stunningly quick leap to the top of the food chain has had enormous consequences. Other alpha animals like lions and sharks evolved slowly over millions of years. This slower development meant that as sharks became deadlier, fish evolved to swim faster. This balanced system never emerged for humans. We evolved to dominate so quickly that both the world and we ourselves didn't have time to adjust.

The ability to control and use fire was the original break point that allowed humans to evolve at hyperspeed. Fire was the first significant differentiator between man and the other animals. By a quarter-million years ago, the forefathers of humans were using fire on a daily basis.[2] Fire was a dependable source of light and warmth, and a deadly weapon against prowling predators. Humans eventually started deliberately burning large swathes of land— a farming practice that is still used around the world today. A controlled burn can turn dense, inhospitable forests into more easily managed terrain full of edible life. The earliest "start-up founders" sifted through the smoking remains of forests, harvested "barbecued" animals, plants, and worms, and brought back the spoils for their tribes.[3]

The most important thing fire did was allow us to control the process of cooking. Richard Wrangham is a Harvard University primatologist who studies wild chimpanzees in Africa. Wrangham knew that cooking is one of the relatively few uniquely human abilities. He also knew that our habit of predigesting our food by heating it allows us to spend less energy on digestion. In the late 1990s, he realized that cooking is not merely the basis of culinary culture; it gave our ancestors a massive evolutionary advantage. "With cooking, we see major adaptive changes," says Wrangham. He argues that cooking paved the way for the dramatic expansion of the human brain and eventually fueled cerebral accomplishments like cave painting, writing, and inventing the Internet.[4]

Foods that humans cannot digest in their natural forms—such as wheat, rice, and potatoes—became staples of our diet, thanks to cooking. Cooking also killed germs and parasites and made it much easier for humans to chew and digest perennial classics like scavenged meat and insects. "What all these adaptations are about is increasing the bang for the buck nutritionally," says William Leonard, a biological anthropologist at Northwestern University.[5]

This all leads to what Wrangham calls "the Cooking Hypothesis." Where chimpanzees spend more than five hours a day chewing raw food, a single hour or less is enough for people eating cooked food. If we ate only raw, unprocessed food, humans would need to eat for 9.3 hours per day in order to fuel our brains, which use about twice as much resting energy by percentage as other primates.[6]

The advent of cooking enabled humans to eat more kinds of food, to devote less time to eating, and to make do with smaller teeth and shorter intestines. Wrangham believes that there is a direct link between the advent of cooking, the shortening of the human intestinal tract, and the growth of the human brain. Since long intestines and large brains are both massive energy consumers, it's hard to have both. By shortening the intestines and decreasing their energy consumption, cooking opened the way to the oversized brains of modern humans.[7] From that point forward, humanity and the world more broadly would never be the same.

From Forager to Farmer

Our modern lives are a direct consequence of how humans evolved and innovated upon the process of cooking and eating. In the grand scheme of history and human evolution, it is not that long ago that

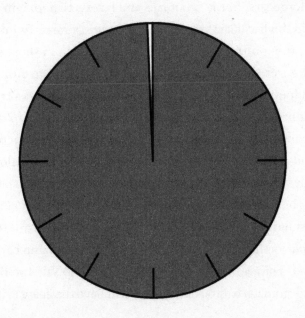

we were all hunter-gatherers, foraging wherever we could find the most food to keep us alive. And our genes passed on to the next generation. The last ten thousand years, during which almost all humans lived as farmers, are a small fraction of the millions of years during which our ancestors hunted and gathered.

Evolutionary psychologists argue that many of our modern social and psychological characteristics were shaped during this long preagricultural era. Even today, our brains and minds are adapted to a life of hunting and gathering. How we cook and eat are the result of the way our hunter-gatherer minds interact with our current postindustrial world. Our modern society gives us more material resources and longer lives than those enjoyed by any previous generation, but it often makes us feel alienated, depressed, and pressured. To understand why, we need to explore the world of our hunter-gatherer ancestors.

Why, for example, do we gorge on high-calorie riskily altered food with little nutritional value that makes us feel bad and is literally killing us? It's a puzzle why we binge on the sweetest and greasiest food we can find, until we consider the eating habits of our forager forebears. In the savannahs and forests that foraging humans inhabited, high-calorie sweets were extremely rare. Twinkies don't exactly grow on trees. Food in general was also in short supply. A typical forager thirty thousand years ago had access to only one type of sweet food—fruit. If a foraging woman came across a tree bursting with bananas, the most biologically rational thing to do was to eat as many of them as she could, before the local group of chimps came and attacked her. The instinct to gorge on high-calorie food, especially high-calorie, very sweet food, is hardwired into our genes.[8]

One hundred thousand years later, we may live in condominiums or suburban mansions, but our genetic memory still thinks we are in fight-or-flight mode. That's why I find it so damn hard to stop at just one Thin Mint Girl Scout cookie—my DNA is yelling at my brain and stomach to stock up while I still have the chance. The presence of these "famine-fighting genes" is widely accepted and is certainly partially responsible for the modern obesity epidemic.[9]

Recent research shows that sugar and sweetness can induce reward and craving sensations that are more powerful than those induced by addictive drugs like cocaine. Although this evidence is limited by the difficulty of comparing rewards and psychological experiences in different humans, it has been supported by recent experimental research on sugar and sweet reward in lab rats.

Overall, this research has revealed that sweet reward can not only substitute for addictive drugs like cocaine but can even be more rewarding and attractive. At the neurobiological level, the behavioral underpinnings in the brain that sugar rewards appear to be more robust than those of cocaine. The research says this "reflects past selective evolutionary pressures for seeking and taking foods high in sugar and calories. The biological robustness in the neural substrates of sugar and sweet reward may be sufficient to explain why many people can have difficulty to control the consumption of foods high in sugar when continuously exposed to them."[10]

Just so we're clear here, research now proves that sugar is more addictive than cocaine—which is pretty insane to think about, especially as we explore in future chapters how the modern food industry is built around jamming as much sugar and sweet as possible into many of the foods we consume every day.

Most foragers lived itinerantly, roaming with their tribe in a constant search for food. They followed seasonal growth cycles and animal migrations, sometimes traveling thousands of miles per year. Most foragers fed themselves as they could, rummaging for bugs, picking berries, burrowing for roots, trapping small animals, and hunting big game. Despite the Hollywood conception of "Man the Hunter," gathering was humans' main activity, and it provided most of their calories.[11]

Foragers also had more stimulating and satisfying lives than farmers or modern-day factory workers. During the preagricultural era, a forager might head out with his friends at nine in the morning. They'd scavenge nearby, gathering nuts, digging up edible bugs, catching snakes, and occasionally sprinting away from predators. Several hours later, they were back at the camp to cook lunch over the fire. That left them plenty of time to tell stories, play with the children, and just hang out.[12]

Humans foraged for millions of years, and the human body was well adapted to it—foraging provided ideal nutrition. Evidence from fossilized skeletons indicates that ancient foragers were less likely to suffer from starvation or malnutrition and were generally taller and healthier than their farmer and factory worker descendants. Average life expectancy was just thirty to forty years, but this was due mostly to the high rate of child mortality. Humans who made it through the hazards of childhood had a good chance of reaching the age of sixty, and some even made it to their eighties.[13]

The foragers were able to stave off both starvation and malnutrition through their varied diet. Especially in premodern times, farmers tended to eat a very limited and unbalanced diet. Most of the calories feeding an agricultural population came from a single crop, like rice, that lacks much of the nutrition humans need.[14]

By contrast, ancient foragers regularly ate dozens of different foods. When you don't know where your next meal will come from and calories are scarce, you become very creative very quickly— necessity is truly the mother of invention and variety. This variety ensured that the ancient foragers received all the necessary nutrients to survive. By not being dependent on any single food source, they were less liable to suffer when one particular food source failed. Agricultural societies, even to this day, are frequently ravaged by famine when crops fail. Foragers definitely suffered from periods of hunger, but they were able to handle such disasters more easily. If they lost some of their staple foods, they could gather or hunt other species or move to a less affected area.[15]

The nutritious and varied diet and the relatively short working week led anthropologists to define preagricultural society as "the original affluent society."[16] But let's not get too caught up with the picturesque visions of hunter-gatherer glory. The truth is that hunter-gatherer societies, like every human society before and since, were very complicated. What we know for sure is that the shift from hunter-gatherer to agricultural society would change our species forever—starting with how we ate and what we cooked.

The Agricultural Revolution

For millions of years, humans ate by gathering wild plants and hunting wild animals—with an emphasis here on *wild*. Our forebears hunted, gathered, and cooked without cultivating or domesticating a single plant or animal. Humans spread from East Africa to the Middle East to Europe and Asia, and finally to Australia and America—but everywhere we went, our ancestors continued to live by gathering wild plants and hunting wild animals. Why do anything else when your lifestyle feeds you more than enough and supports a rich world of social structures, religious beliefs, and political dynamics?[17]

All this changed about ten thousand years ago, when humans abandoned hunting and gathering in exchange for farming. Our great-great-grandparents (raised to the two-hundredth power) believed that cultivation, planting, and herding would provide them with more food and better lives. The Agricultural Revolution was a literal revolution in the way humans lived.

The Agricultural Revolution started around 9000 B.C. in what is today modern Turkey, Syria, and Iran. Wheat and goats were domesticated by approximately 9000 B.C.; peas and lentils around 8000 B.C.; olive trees by 5000 B.C.; horses by 4000 B.C.; and grapevines by 3500 B.C. Today, more than 90 percent of the calories that feed humanity come from the handful of plants that our ancestors domesticated between 9500 and 3500 B.C.——wheat, rice, corn, potatoes, millet, and barley. No noteworthy plant or animal has been domesticated in the last two thousand years. From the Middle East, agriculture spread far and wide. By the first century A.D., the vast majority of people throughout most of the world were farmers. As historical anthropologist Yuval Harari recounts, "If our minds are those of hunter-gatherers, our cuisine is that of ancient farmers."[18]

Historians once believed that the Agricultural Revolution was a massive advance for humankind. The narrative goes something like this: "Evolution gradually produced ever more intelligent people. Eventually, people were so smart that they were able to decipher nature's secrets, enabling them to tame sheep and cultivate wheat. As soon as this happened, they cheerfully abandoned the grueling, dangerous, and often spartan life of hunter-gatherers, settling down to enjoy the pleasant, satiated life of farmers."[19]

That idyllic vision is nothing more than a modern Excel slave's bucolic fantasy. Instead of bringing a new era of better living, the Agricultural Revolution brought farmers more difficult and less satisfying lives than those of foragers. Hunter-gatherers spent their time on more interesting and diverse activities and were in less danger of starvation. The Agricultural Revolution increased the amount of food at the disposal of humans, but the extra food did not always translate into better nutrition or more freedom. Instead, this extra food led to population explosions and wealth accumulation for a select few, those who would become the kings, emperors, and priests. The average farmer worked harder and longer than the average forager and in return received a worse diet and a worse life. As *Guns, Germs, and Steel* author Jared Diamond would put it, the Agricultural Revolution was history's biggest fraud.[20]

Some argue that the handful of plants that humans purportedly domesticated actually domesticated *us*. It is these plants (wheat, rice, corn, potatoes, millet, and barley) that transformed us from nutritionally balanced, freely roaming foragers into the forebears for obesity, diabetes, and deskbound death.

At the start of the Agricultural Revolution, wheat was just a wild grass confined to a small range in the Middle East. By the advent of Christianity, it was growing all over the world. According to the basic evolutionary criteria of survival and reproduction, wheat has become one of the most successful plants in the history of the earth. In areas such as the Great Plains, where not a single wheat stalk grew ten thousand years ago, you can today walk for hundreds upon hundreds of miles without encountering any other plant. Worldwide, wheat covers about 870,000 square miles of the globe's surface, an area slightly larger than Saudi Arabia.[21]

For twenty-first-century Americans, corn is even more of a modern miracle of domestication. It's one we take for granted every day, multiple times per day—because in some way, shape, or form, corn has found its way into almost everything we eat. And that is not a good thing. But more on that in the next chapter. For now, how did this bizarre Mexican grass go from the obscure to the omnipresent?

A Corny History

Ten thousand years ago, the earliest Mexicans were learning how to master maize, or what we call corn. Scientists working during the first part of the twentieth century uncovered evidence that they believed linked maize to what, at first glance, would seem to be a very unlikely parent: a Mexican grass called teosinte.[22] Researchers discovered that all maize was genetically most similar to a type of teosinte from the tropical Central Balsas River Valley of southern Mexico, suggesting that this region was the cradle of corn evolution. By calculating the genetic distance between modern maize and

Balsas teosinte, they estimated that domestication occurred about nine thousand years ago.[23]

The most crucial step in the domestication process was freeing the teosinte kernels from their stony cases. Another step was developing plants where the kernels remained intact on the cobs, unlike the teosinte ears, which shatter into individual kernels. Early cultivators had to notice among their stands of plants variants in which the nutritious kernels were at least partially exposed, or whose ears held together better, or that had more rows of kernels, and they had to selectively breed them. It is estimated that the initial domestication process that produced the maize that forms the basis of what we know today required a few thousand years.[24]

Within a couple of millennia, humans in many parts of the world were doing little from dawn to dusk other than taking care of corn. From clearing to plowing to picking to watering and fighting off pesky animals and bugs, humans had not evolved for such tasks. We were adapted to climbing trees, killing snakes, and burrowing for bugs, not to farming. Even more disruptive, farming required so much time and diligence that people were forced to live next to their cornfields—forever. Over the course of a couple of thousand years, we went from climbing trees to cleaning corncobs.

Corn convinced ancient Americans to exchange a relatively good and freedom-filled life for a more miserable and domesticated existence. Corn did not offer a better diet. Wild grains made up only a small fraction of the human diet before the Agricultural Revolution, and a diet based on any one grain is nutritionally poor. Corn didn't help people gain more food security either. Farmers rely on a small number of plants for their livelihood, and if those plants fail, the farmers tend to fail as well. And failure for farmers was no hasty retreat from a marauding savannah lion—rather it often meant widespread famine and death. And farming corn also didn't lead to a reduction in intertribal violence. Actually, it was just the opposite. As farmers literally and proverbially planted seeds, they acquired more stuff. Instead of being able to pack up and move camp at the sign of violence like foragers, farmers had to fight in order to defend their homes, fields, equipment, and food stores.[25]

Agriculture offered very little for humans as individuals, but farming was a great leap forward for humans as a species. Farming allowed the human population to boom by growing more food per square foot than was ever possible without cultivation. More food meant more people. Humans were sicker and less happy, but we were able to multiply—and that is ultimately how you win the game of evolution. Winning for a modern-day business is defined by scale and growth. The same is true for the evolutionary success of humanity. If a species stops expanding and multiplying, eventually it goes extinct, just as a company without profits and growth eventually goes bankrupt.

This is the essence of the Agricultural Revolution: the ability to keep more people alive under worse conditions. Yet why should individuals care about this evolutionary calculus? Why would any sane person lower his or her standard of living just to multiply the number of copies of the human genome? Nobody agreed to this deal: The Agricultural Revolution was a trap.[26]

The CRAP Trap

As more effort was directed toward cultivation, there was less time to hunt and gather, and the foragers became farmers. By 8500 B.C., Mexico and parts of the modern-day United States were peppered with permanent villages that were tied to corn farming.[27]

With the move to permanent villages and the increase in food supply, the population soared. Babies were fed on corn porridge in addition to breast milk, which meant that women could have more children. As people began living in disease-ridden settlements, as children fed more on cereals and less on mother's milk, and as each child competed for his or her food with more and more siblings, child mortality soared. In most agricultural societies, at least one out of every three children died before reaching twenty. Yet the increase in births still outpaced the increase in deaths; humans kept having larger numbers of children.[28]

The average person in 5,000 B.C. lived a harder life than the average person in 15,000 B.C. It's pretty wild to think that ten thousand years of evolution and "progress" actually led to a regression in happiness and health. But our ancestors didn't realize what was happening. Small changes and "improvements" that were supposed to make life easier and better actually made life much worse.

Does this sound familiar? To me, it sounds a lot like what happened over the course of the twentieth century, which we'll get to in a few pages. As the Agricultural Revolution unfolded, the promise and pursuit of an easier, better, more convenient life actually resulted in unhappiness, stress, and poor health. This same process afflicts us today.

When I left the Marine Corps, I drank the Kool-Aid and went to Wall Street. I told myself I would work hard to earn money and that by the time I was forty I would retire to pursue my passions. However, what I saw on the trading desk disabused me of this vision. The forty-year-olds on my trading floor had seven-figure mortgages, children in private schools, multiple cars with expensive monthly lease obligations, and a general addiction to the finer things in life that is commonly referred to as the Goldman handcuffs. And it's not entirely their fault. What are they supposed to do, go back to farming?

One of the beautiful curses of being human is that we can adapt to anything, both good and bad. This is good because it allowed my dad's family to survive Nazi concentration camps and long periods of starvation and hardship. This is bad because convenience becomes routine—we get used to a certain luxury, and eventually, we take it for granted. We'll talk about this more in chapter 9 when we discuss the hedonic treadmill. Eventually, we reach a point where we can't live without it. Processed foods are the perfect example of what I call the CRAP Trap.

Over the last fifty years, fast food was invented to make life easier and better. Previously, it took a lot of work to plant, nurture, and grow food, harvest it, take it to market, barter, shop, carry it home, prepare it, cook it, and serve it warm to your family. It took months to run this process from end to end. The advent of the drive-through allowed us to get food without all the hassle in a matter of minutes. We've saved all that trouble and time, but do we live a more relaxed, healthier, happier life? We definitely save time, but few would argue that it's worth the ultimate price we pay.

Today, the occasional antitechnologist refuses to shop at a grocery store or eat at a restaurant, just as historically some humans refused to farm. But the Agricultural Revolution didn't need every tribe to take part. It only needed one. Once one group settled down and started cultivating, whether in the Middle East or Mexico, agriculture was unstoppable. Since farming led to massive population growth, farmers had more bodies and hands to fight against hunter-gatherers. The foragers could either run away or start farming themselves.[29]

The story of the CRAP Trap is the story of how we allowed food to become so broken. Our search for an easier life transformed the world in ways nobody could imagine. Nobody planned the Agricultural Revolution or our dependence on farming. Many small decisions aimed at filling our stomachs more conveniently had the cumulative effect of forcing our ancestors to be less healthy and happy. As monumental as the Agricultural Revolution was, the twenty-first-century Industrial Food Revolution would change the face (and waistline) of humanity in an even more dramatic way.

Eating Evolution, Part 2: The Birth of Big Food

One-liner: How did we get so disconnected from our kitchens and our food?

How did food in America get so broken? How did we go from foraging to farming to fatty liver disease? The one-line answer is this: Over the last century, a deadly misalignment has grown between the food industry's incentives and our desires and needs as humans.

I am an avowed capitalist, and I love building companies, because I think there is no more efficient way to create the products and services that will impact and change the world.

But the food industry's development and evolution over the twentieth century, the Industrial Food Revolution, is emblematic of how capitalism and humanity can sometimes be at odds and how success can lead to failure.

Let's explore the last century and how we got so disconnected from cooking, and our food, and how that disconnect produced our current Flawed American Diet (FAD).

The Origins of Big Food

Up front, it's important to understand that Big Food companies and the people who run them are *not* evil. These enormous companies were built over the last century to do something very important: to make safe food more convenient and accessible. Every revolution has unexpected fallout, and though definitions of safety and accessibility have shifted, many corporations have failed to keep up. Many face massive challenges to change how they operate due to consumer and shareholder demands and institutional inertia. Going from sixty to zero in a Ferrari is easy. Doing the same with an intergalactic space cruiser takes a lot longer.

For Big Food, people eating fresh food at home is an obstacle to selling more of its products. Big Food makes money by changing food culture and food traditions through developing its own rituals and traditions. For the last century, this has consisted of getting people to eat the highly processed and riskily altered provisions that Big Food became world class at making. But no one should be eating Fritos multiple times per week, let alone multiple times per day. Once you have changed people's taste buds, you have changed the way they eat.

So who and what exactly is Big Food?

Big Food is the companies that make up the multitrillion-dollar industry that grows, raises, slaughters, manufactures, packages, and sells most of the food Americans eat. Think of Big Food as four different levels of a riskily altered food pyramid.

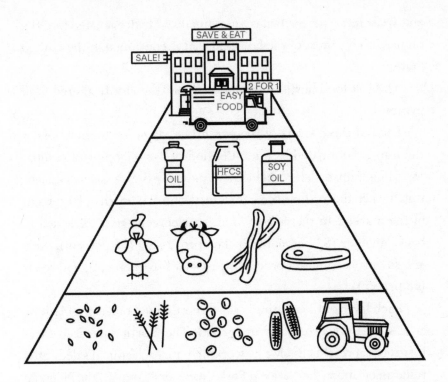

The base of the pyramid is Big Agriculture, or the input producers, the companies that until consolidation accelerated in the
1980s were family-owned farms. Today, this is primarily the corn
and soybean megafarms of the Midwest. This base also includes the
multibillion-dollar oligopoly of companies that supply all farmers
with seeds and chemicals.

The input producers create and sell the stuff that Big Meat buys,
the next level up the pyramid. This is another multibillion-dollar
oligopoly of companies that raise, slaughter, and process most of the
cows, chickens, and pigs that Americans eat.

The next level up the pyramid is the consumer packaged goods
(CPG) industry. This is where the raw ingredients are processed and
transformed into the fundamental elements of riskily altered provisions. Corn is chemically altered into high-fructose corn syrup using acid enzymes with such family-friendly names as *alpha-amylase*

and *xylose isomerase*. Soybeans are refined and hydrogenated into the oil used to fry most of the fast food that is consumed in the United States.

The fast-food hustlers are at the top of the riskily altered food pyramid.

Each of these layers of the pyramid (except for the retailers at the top) is dominated by a multibillion-dollar oligopoly of companies. Economists determine that an industry is excessively concentrated when the top four companies in it control more than 40 percent of the market. In the case of food, that percentage is exceeded in beef slaughter (82 percent), chicken processing (53 percent), corn and soy processing (85 percent), pesticides (62 percent), and seeds (58 percent).[1]

Each layer of the pyramid is also represented on Capitol Hill by at least one powerful lobbying group. The North American Meat Institute represents Big Meat, working with each animal's dedicated trade association (the National Pork Producers Council, the National Cattlemen's Beef Association, and the National Chicken Council). The American Farm Bureau Federation lobbies for the growers of commodity crops. The National Restaurant Association is the voice of the fast-food chains. CropLife America speaks for the pesticide industry.[2]

These lobbying groups push for legislation (or lack thereof) on their own, but they also often work together as one very powerful voice in Washington on such issues as crop subsidies or the labeling of genetically modified food. In recent years, the various layers of the pyramid have been cemented together through the appearance of a common enemy: consumers recognizing that market concentration is dangerous, especially when it comes to food. So while it is a simplification, it still makes sense to talk about Big Food as a single powerful entity.[3]

The ten biggest food corporations employ over seven hundred thousand people and account for almost $300 billion in annual sales.[4]

Almost all these companies and the brands they launched date back to the last century. Oreo, for example, now owned by Mondelez International, was launched in 1912 and has sold over five hundred billion cookies since it was introduced to cookie-craving American consumers. The scale, reach, and power of these companies is hard to fathom. PepsiCo's sales from food alone are bigger than more than half of the GDP of the world's countries that are recognized by the United Nations. When you add PepsiCo's beverage sales to the mix, they are bigger than two-thirds of all countries' combined GDPs.[5] But it wasn't always this way.

A Century of Change

The world has changed dramatically over the last hundred years. In 1915, the Great War's battles were being fought in Europe using bayonets and single-shot rifles, where on a regular basis, tens of thousands of soldiers would die—in a single day. Electricity was just entering the mainstream, and electric refrigeration was still decades away. Fewer than 10 percent of families owned a car. Airplanes were still a highly dubious proposition capable of carrying one or two people, flying only a few miles at a time. Escalators, tea bags, instant coffee, and disposable razor blades were all cutting-edge innovations. It was a very different time and a very different world.

Thanks to advances in technology that were applied across dozens of industries, food became safer, better, and cheaper. The average American household's spending on food went from 42 percent to less than 15 percent of annual income. In 1915, the average farmer fed about 15 people. Today, he feeds more than 120. American agriculture in the twenty-first century is a marvel of modern science and economics. The bottom line for most families is that our wealth has grown multiples faster than the price of food.[6]

Food is one of the most critical issues currently facing America and the world. Where we go from here will determine not only the quality and length of our individual lives but also the future of the planet as we know it.

First, if we don't change how we produce, distribute, and consume food, eventually we will not have a planet to call home. The overwhelming scientific consensus is that global warming is real and very dangerous. You can make all the jokes you want about cow farts, but methane is twenty times more potent than CO_2. Livestock (particularly cows) produce methane as part of the enteric fermentation in their digestion, and methane makes up 30 percent of the greenhouse gas emissions from agriculture. And it's not just methane and livestock. Agriculture is also one of the biggest culprits in land degradation, air and water pollution, water shortages, and loss of biodiversity.

We live on a planet of 7.3 billion people, where even today some 2 billion people do not have enough to eat. Moreover, by 2050, the total population is projected to grow to almost 10 billion people. Another billion or so people will enter the middle class in that time, radically accelerating their demand for calories in the form of meat, fish, milk, eggs, and other energy-dense foods. The Food and Agriculture Organization of the United Nations projects that the world's farmers will have to produce 70 percent more calories by 2050, on less land (perhaps much less land) and with less water than they do today.

The way we produce food, and the amount and way we eat today, will not scale to feed ten billion.[7]

Second, much of the food that is produced and distributed in America today is not aimed primarily at nutrition. When you engineer salt, fat, and sugar, foods become incredibly attractive—and addictive. The right food processing will kick off the same dopamine network that triggers cravings that are more powerful than a drug addict's. And we see the consequences. One hundred million Americans are now diabetic or prediabetic. And type 2 diabetes, which used to be called adult onset diabetes, is now afflicting children. In 1980, you could not find a child with type 2 diabetes.

Diabetes, heart disease, stroke, and some cancers are diseases that are far more prevalent in the United States than anywhere in the rest of the world. And that's the direct result of eating a Western diet, the Flawed American Diet (FAD).[8] These are diseases that either did not exist or were much rarer prior to the advent of industrialized American farming and food production.

Our demand for meat, dairy, and refined carbohydrates drives us to consume way more calories than are good for us. Far more Americans die from overconsumption than from underconsumption (a.k.a. hunger), even while millions of our children go hungry and fill up on chips and soda. If every drop of Coke consumed per year in the United States alone was put in sixteen-ounce bottles and laid end to end, they would reach the moon and back—several dozen times.[9] And those calories are in foods and beverages that cause, not prevent, disease.

Reconnect with Your Food

If you care about the world your children will inherit, and how well and long you are going to live in that world, you should probably be thinking about where your food is coming from, what's in it, and how it is being raised or produced.

Eating fresh, real food is the best way to both connect to where your food is coming from and to ensure that you and your family are eating only high-quality, sustainable, healthy ingredients.

The current food-driven health crisis was entirely preventable. Grandma could have stopped it by sticking to her cooking (and knitting), but market forces conspired against her. We were assured that the more Spam we ate and the more Coke we drank, the healthier and happier we'd be. But the opposite truth has played out.

What do cows and Coke have in common? Beyond being a bit gassy (sorry, I couldn't resist), they both have also been marketed heavily by Big Food, creating unnatural demand. We're not born craving Big Macs and Sprite, but their production and distribution have been supported by government subsidies at the expense of a more earth- and waistline-friendly diet.

Eating Like Your Grandma Did Is Really Hard

A hundred years ago, every American ate locally and sustainably, because there was no other option. Even my hometown of New York was still surrounded by farms, and shipping food all over the country was a ridiculous notion because interstate highways and trucks didn't exist, and refrigeration consisted of blocks of ice covered in sawdust. Most women of that era were discouraged from holding jobs outside of the house, so instead, they spent their days buying food in the local market and preparing it at home.[10]

Back in those days, before Michael Pollan and Julia Child and Jamie Oliver, there was no philosophy of food. You just ate, probably as your parents and their parents had eaten for hundreds of years. Food didn't define you, it fueled you. There were few national brands, most foods had no labels, and there was little to no marketing. Daily vitamins and supplements had not been invented, and there were no health claims outside of the snake oil salesmen. You didn't think about "groups" or "pyramids" or "diets" or fats, carbs, and proteins. You ate what your mom put on your plate.

Hardly anything contained more than a few ingredients, at most. Americans grew real food, and they ate real food. And again, everyone ate local, because there was no alternative. Tang, Wheaties, Snickers, Gatorade, Spam, Nathan's hot dogs—none of these had been invented yet. Today, it's hard to imagine American culture without these icons.

Farm subsidies changed everything. During the Great Depression and Dust Bowl, Presidents Hoover and Roosevelt argued that nonfarmers must be taxed so that farmers, the backbone of the American economy at the time, could be supported. My family in South Dakota received these subsidies—without them, I probably wouldn't be here today.

However, once some farmers had their subsidies, they were viewed as entitlements and were hard to take away, even when the farm crises of the Great Depression and Dust Bowl were over. Then these subsidies were used to reduce the cost of feed production, which resulted in a flooding of the market with artificially cheap products, primarily corn and soy. Many of the problems with the FAD today were created by American food policies that were developed during the Great Depression.

From the 1950s onward, President Eisenhower built the interstate highway system, trucks took the place of railroads, and fresh food began to travel farther and farther. Once-exotic produce like oranges became common in New York, California became an agricultural hub, and suburbs took over farmland. Eventually, California produced too much food to ship fresh, so it became critical to process, package, and market canned and frozen foods. Thus arrived America's first flirtations with "fast food." It was marketed to "modern housewives" as a way to cut down on housework. The effects of this move to convenience and industrialization are well known, and they are omnipresent in the America we know today.

From K Rations to CRAP

For far too long, cooking was women's responsibility. There was a very clear division of labor. Even in many traditional societies where men were out hunting, women were doing the cooking. This was certainly true in the United States.

By post–World War II–era America, we no longer had tribes or extended families. Instead, cooking and eating were done at the nuclear-family level. Women found themselves alone and isolated in the kitchen for the first time in human history.

Cooking had moved from communal activity to chore.

When I lived in Java in 2006 and 2007, I would visit the local market with my host mom and her friends. We would chat with the vendors selling everything from dried chili peppers to dozens of varieties of rice to freshly slaughtered beef, where the flies competed with the housewives to see who could "steak" a claim first. She would select what she wanted along with her friends, and they would bring home the fresh provisions and spend most of the morning communally preparing dishes together for lunch and dinner. Food gathering, preparation, and cooking looked a lot like this all over the world for the previous ten thousand years.

As food preparation in the United States became more of a solitary endeavor, women found themselves spending much of their time and a lot of their day alone. The social and tribal relationship humans had to cooking for millions of years had been broken. The typical way the story is told is that the feminist revolution came, women went to work, and they stopped cooking. And that was the end of cooking in America.

But it's a somewhat more complicated story, and Big Food played a crucial role in the downfall of cooking culture. Beginning after World War II, the commercialization of processed and shelf-stable food first invented for military applications made its way into the mainstream.

Big Food put a lot of effort into selling Americans on the processed food wonders that it had invented to feed the troops. Canned meals, freeze-dried foods, dehydrated potatoes, powdered orange juice, and instant coffee——these were the items found in the typical K ration.

The K ration was an individual daily combat food ration that was introduced by the United States Army during World War II.

It was originally intended as an individually packaged daily ration for issue to airborne troops, the tank corps, motorcycle couriers, and other mobile forces for short durations of intense movement and activity. The K ration would evolve—if you can call it that—over time to become the MREs that I consumed while living for weeks on end in the desert with the Marine Corps.

What was designed for durability and short-term nutrition for soldiers, sailors, and marines in combat was repackaged and marketed toward housewives as perpetual convenience.

These products changed thousands of years of food traditions. The shift toward industrial food production, accelerated food processing, and convenient consumption was a supply-driven phenomenon. Consumers weren't at first demanding Tang, Spam, and microwave dinners. Instead, the food companies came out of World War II, with demand from the armed forces essentially gone overnight. Millions of soldiers, sailors, and marines returned to civilian life and their wives and families. Food industry executives of the late 1940s had to figure out innovative distribution and marketing approaches in order to keep selling their newly invented products, and the natural place to move those products was into people's kitchens.[11] The idea was to market new products in many different ways that would teach consumers new rituals and behaviors in order to get them to buy more and make their lives easier.

By midcentury, we were hooked on hundreds of processed-food ingredients that did not exist prior to World War II. Again, keep in mind that the major food challenge of the 1950s was safety, accessibility, and convenience. Food processing accomplished this masterfully.

This was a win for Big Food (more money), a win for the consumer (new and exciting products), and a win for society (more people getting the safely delivered calories they needed than at any point before in human history). But it turns out that there was a pernicious downside to processed food that we didn't come to understand until it was too late.

A CRAPpy Spectrum

First, let's define what we're talking about. Processed food has a bad reputation as a diet destroyer. It has been roundly blamed for our nation's obesity epidemic, high blood pressure, and the prevalence of type 2 diabetes. But processed food is more than Oreos and Cheetos, Lay's and McDonald's hamburgers. It may be a surprise to learn that guacamole, homemade salad, or sautéed carrots are also technically processed foods.

We have to determine what *processed* really means when we're talking about processed food. There is a significant difference between a food being *riskily altered* and a food being *processed*. Keep in mind that as a cook, you're doing processing yourself—think about using a food processor. Is that dangerous and bad for your health and waistline? We get caught up and confused by the word *processed* without realizing what it truly means.

The Spectrum of CRAP (Consumable Riskily Altered Provisions): Processed food falls on a spectrum from minimally to heavily processed. Again, the operative words are "riskily altered."

- *Minimally processed and not riskily altered foods—such as bagged spinach, cut vegetables, and roasted nuts—are often simply preprepped for convenience.*

- *Foods processed at their peak to lock in nutritional quality and freshness include canned beans, tomatoes, frozen fruit and vegetables, and canned tuna.*

- *Light CRAP: Foods made with riskily altered ingredients added for flavor and texture (sweeteners, spices, oils, colors, and preservatives) include jarred pasta sauce, salad dressing, yogurt, and cake mixes.*

- *CRAP: Ready-to-eat foods—such as potato chips, granola, and deli meat—are more heavily processed.*

- *Heavy CRAP: The most heavily processed foods often are shelf-stable or premade meals, including MREs, frozen pizza, and microwaveable dinners.*

I define Consumable Riskily Altered Provisions as foods that have been chemically processed and made solely or mainly from refined ingredients and artificial substances. Obviously, most of the food we eat is processed in some way—oranges are picked from trees, butter is churned, fish is caught. But there's a massive difference between mechanical and chemical processing. If it's a single ingredient with no added chemicals, then it's okay if it has been ground up and put in a jar—it's real food. If the ingredients or the entire meal have been chemically enhanced or processed, then it has been riskily altered.

It's worth noting here that I am not an ideologue or a purist. I love Kettle Brand jalapeño potato chips. I love Samoa Girl Scout cookies. And I love Snickers. I'm talking, like, really *love* here, man.

But I know what I'm getting into. And it is totally okay to indulge, as indulgence allows us to live fully—that's why we sell desserts at Plated. But no one should be eating riskily altered foods multiple times per day, every day of the week—and that's what Big Food wants us to do.

Cost and Craving

"The transition of food to being an industrial product really has been a fundamental problem," says Walter Willett, the chair of Harvard's

Department of Nutrition. "First, the actual processing has stripped away the nutritional value of the food. Most of the grains have been converted to starches. We have sugar in concentrated form, and many of the fats have been concentrated and then, worst of all, hydrogenated, which creates trans-fatty acids with very adverse effects on health."[12]

David Cutler from Harvard and Julia Wolfson from Johns Hopkins have done extensive research correlating rates of cooking and rates of obesity. They found that as the amount of time we spend cooking goes down, the rate of obesity goes up. Put differently, as the time-cost of food goes down, or as you can eat food without putting time into gathering and preparing it, you eat more of it.

As we saw in chapter 1, as humans, we have an innate, hard-wired desire to cook. However, the CRAP Trap pushes us away from our better instincts.

What's driving the increase in obesity, especially among children? Simple answer: The ubiquity of inexpensive, mouthwatering, super-sized, energy-dense riskily altered foods.

We are eating unhealthy, high-labor, high–time consumption foods that are delivered cheaply and conveniently. Think about potato chips. If you were to make your own potato chips from scratch, you would have to wash, peel, fry, and air-dry potatoes before you could even get to the seasoning and noshing. But that's not what happens today. Instead, you pop open the bag, and five hundred calories later, you're sitting on the couch, crying salty chip tears while watching the most recent Ryan Gosling movie on Netflix.[13]

My philosophy is this: You can eat whatever you want, but it should be real and fresh whenever possible.

Probably the biggest problem with cooking is that if you have a limited amount of money and you go into the supermarket, you will find yourself gravitating to the middle aisles, where all the processed food is located, and away from the produce section, which tends to be on the perimeter of the store. And the reason for this is that over

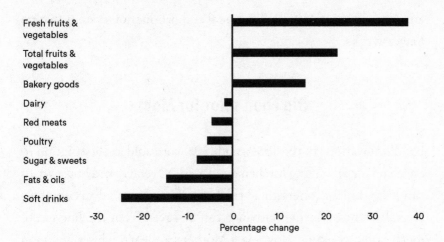

the last half century, produce has gotten a lot more expensive and processed food has not.

The average price of soda since 1985 is down 25 percent. The average price of fresh fruits and veggies over the same period is up 40 percent.[14] And that coincides one for one with the obesity and diabetes epidemics. If you are looking to get as many calories as you can for one dollar, your best bet is processed food. However, that's not saying you're getting the most nutrition for your dollar. Quite the opposite.

Big Food's business model optimizes for two things: cost and craving.

To make a new chip guaranteed to create a craving requires calculus and advanced mapping tools. The objective is to find what Big Food calls the "bliss point," or the precise amount of processing that triggers an opiate-like response from consumers. The bliss point is then forced onto a cost curve, where different ingredient inputs are traded in order to obtain the highest possible bliss for the lowest possible cost. It bears repeating once again:

The people who run the Big Food companies are not evil. They are just boxed into a business model and production system that no longer works.

Big Food's Hot for Mom

Food innovations in the 1950s and '60s were sold as the solution to once and for all ending kitchen drudgery. "Overworked housewives can relax until dinnertime," read one TV dinner advertisement. "Equally long-suffering husbands can be saved from the horrors of much home cooking. Now even Mother can learn what's going on in the outside world. She doesn't even have to don an apron."[15]

The food companies targeted busy housewives, building up the idea that life at home was some horrible existence between solitary indentured servitude and a constant state of panic. You can see the drumbeat across all the food advertising of the period. The mantra was save time, savor the convenience, and "This is better than what you can make yourself at home."

In the 1960s and '70s, as women were working in greater numbers, a new conversation started between men and women. It was clear that there needed to be a new division of labor in the household—women couldn't work, and take care of the kids, and clean the house, and do the shopping and cooking. There were public and private fights about this, and some domestic modifications began to happen. But before American society could complete that renegotiation, Big Food stepped forward and said, "Stop the fussing and fighting! We've got your back! We'll do the cooking for you."

You see this vividly in an advertising campaign that Kentucky Fried Chicken launched in the 1970s. It was a brilliant move on the part of KFC to align corporate profit–driven interests with the homemaker aspirations of working women and the masculine hunter-type, eat-or-be-eaten pressure on men to solve the perennial dinner dilemma.

As Kentucky Fried Chicken sales began to skyrocket, more and more food companies moved toward food processing as a means to drive both top- and bottom-line numbers while delivering solutions for millions of confused and time-starved moms.

And that ushered in the situation that we find ourselves in now, where Big Food deliberately discredits cooking as an everyday practice and art. Food marketers bend over backward to convince us that cooking is really hard, really time-consuming, and really messy and that we'd all be much better off using convenient processed shortcuts.

Fast food and other convenient foods may have reduced household chores, but they also diminished the variety and nutritional content of the food Americans ate. This was the CRAP Trap baring its ugly fangs. Most of my parents' generation grew up never eating a fresh vegetable except the occasional broccoli or iceberg lettuce salad. Veggies could go play with the Commies—blue-blooded Americans wanted to eat meat out of a can.

Meat, Meat, Meat

America of the 1950s, '60s, and '70s was all about meat. We had won the Second World War, we were the most powerful country in the world, and we had enough wealth and stability to eat meat three meals a day for the first time in human history.

What could be easier, "healthier," and more American for your family than bacon for breakfast, ham for lunch, and steak for dinner?

By the 1970s, this resulted in unnatural cattle-raising practices. Rather than spending their lives eating grass, for which their stomachs were designed, cows were forced to eat the artificially cheaper (due to subsidies) soy and corn. Ruminants have trouble digesting those grains, and as farms got larger and space more constrained, the cows became increasingly sicker and sicker. So new drugs were invented and deployed to keep the herd healthy. Well, they kept them alive, but healthy is another story. Today, 80 percent of antibiotics in the United States are not administered to people but to animals.[16]

And with the plethora of government subsidies and the resulting rise of industrial farming, a cycle of dietary and planetary destruction began. Meat consumption increased fivefold.[17]

More subsidies led to cheaper production costs, which led to less expensive food, which created what is today the fast-food industry.

Home cooking remained the norm for a while, but as more and more women entered the workforce, there were fewer meals made from scratch. Any and all premade meats, salads, soups, potatoes, and more could be bought at any grocery store or fast-food drive-through. In the process, an entire generation of women (and men) didn't learn how to prepare or appreciate real, fresh food.

Just like any other manufacturing process, food was now being raised and assembled without deeper connection or emotional thought. As a consequence, we became disconnected from the emotion of a good home-cooked meal.

Sadly, it was at this time that the prototypical family dinner began its long slide. This was the peak of process-enriched and preservative-enhanced food, which contained as many soy and corn products as could be packed into it.

The Big Food business model depends on getting the cheapest possible raw ingredients and making them as attractive as cost effectively possible. When you let Big Food cook your food, it cooks differently from the way normal people do. You can tell just by reading the ingredient label. You don't have monoglycerides and diglycerides in your pantry. You don't have high-fructose corn syrup in your pantry.

The infamous chicken nugget is a great example. Tens of millions of chickens are raised and fattened in feedlots that stretch for dozens of miles, where they are force-fed corn. Their meat is ground up and mixed with more corn products and preservatives to help it all stick together and have good mouthfeel. The nuggets are then pre-fried in an industrial corn oil bath so that all you, the "chef," have to do at home is stick those bad boys in the microwave. But yet again, the CRAP Trap has its costs.

By the 1980s, fresh food was in such a sad state that the high fat and salt contents of foods like chicken nuggets and Spam made these fake foods more appealing than the bland dishes that people had previously cooked at home, like broccoli. Millions of women were working and had less time available, and fresh food simply wasn't viewed as important enough for men to change their habits and share the burden.

One Giant Leap Forward, One Evolutionary Step Back

Women entering the workforce was a massive leap forward for humanity, but the way Big Food enabled our adaptation to this change from a caloric consumption perspective was a step backward in human evolution. For many time-strapped families, instead of a home-cooked nutritious meal, dinner became pizza delivery, microwave nuggets, or fast food at the drive-through. During the years when both of my parents were working full-time with seven kids to feed, we were definitely not eating home-cooked meals from scratch many weeknights.

If you are a student of American history or food, none of this should be revelatory or revolutionary. But why should it matter?

THE ENVIRONMENT

As food-activist chef Dan Barber wrote, "The warnings are clear: because we eat in a way that undermines . . . and abuses natural resources (to say nothing of the economic and social implications), the conventional food system cannot be sustained."[18]

But leading with an environmental argument is tough. We rarely see and feel the environmental consequences of our actions soon enough to change our behaviors.

OUR HEALTH AND HAPPINESS

Our waistlines, blood biomarkers, and emotional well-being, on the other hand, we can measure and feel every day, minute by minute. Our health and happiness are perhaps the most direct and unfortunate casualties of the CRAP Trap.

Why is it impossible for the incumbent food companies to lead the way on change? I guess I shouldn't have been surprised, but I was taken aback to speak with current and former employees from Big Food, who described how incredibly averse the CPG giants are to taking risks. Geoff Bible, the former CEO at Philip Morris, described what it would take for a Kraft brand manager about come up with a "better for you" peanut butter.

Essentially, the employee would have to put his or her career on the line to bring a healthier product to market because the risk of failure is so high. Despite platitudes about innovation, Big Food first and foremost needs to preserve profits.

So instead they resort to uninspiring tweaks (think omega-3-infused peanut butter) and line extensions (peanut butter and jelly in the same jar!), which are a far cry from invention and imagining new ways for people to eat better, even at Nestlé with their 350 Ph.D. food scientists.

The Big Food business model that unconsciously evolved over the course of the twenty-first century focuses on convenience and cost to the exclusion of connection, experience, health, and sustainability. We started Plated because we knew there had to be a better way.

Our Fourth Core Belief is: *Food, and the experiences of choosing it, cooking it, and sharing it, are to be celebrated, and thoughtful design in all things is an essential part of that celebration.* While our business model is technology-driven, we deploy innovation in support of the fundamentally human experience of cooking and sharing food. Over the following chapters, we will see what happens when food production is cleaved away from the experience of preparing and sharing.

Picture of an Evolved Eater

Leslie Fiet, Salt Lake City, Utah

I'm a typical product of someone born in 1970. I'm an entrepreneur, and as a single mother, I found myself living on welfare in dead-end jobs at the age of twenty-two after a very bad marriage. I looked at myself in my blue polyester uniform working at the grocery store, and I said, "This is not me." I kicked myself in the butt.

In 2007, I opened Utah's first cupcake shop. I wanted to bake from scratch since so much of what we eat is processed crap. The way we eat forces people to go on diets, to make bad food choices. I called my business Mini's Cupcakes because the cupcakes are smaller, more of a European model. I was so appalled by the McDonald's "supersize me" phase that I wanted to do something to fight it.

And that's part of why we love Plated. Before Plated, dinner was easy and fast, but without thought, we'd whip something up on the stove or in the microwave like spaghetti, then my kids were off to the basement to watch TV. We never had dinner together. The only time we sat down together was Sunday.

We have two kids at home, and I work from 6:00 A.M. to 6:00 P.M. *I wanted dinner not to be painful.* I wanted great dinner, and I didn't want to have to think about it. I hated the waste, and I hate, hate, hate going to the grocery store. I could never find that one stupid ingredient I needed, like fish sauce, then I'd end up buying a whole bottle when all I needed was a teaspoon. Then I'd find that bottle four months later, and I'd end up throwing the whole thing away—*I hate that!*

Plated has opened up a whole new dinner experience for us. For a meal of Plated quality, we're not going to waste that experience sitting in front of the television. We eat more slowly now, because we're talking together over dinner. We turn off the TV, the kids set the dinner table, they ask what's for dinner, they help out, even my husband, who has no idea how to cook. I mean, he thinks cooking is ordering pizza, but even he has made a dozen meals by this point. So we all cook together, then we just sit and eat and talk. I'm learning things about my family that I never knew before, that I never had time to learn before. Unless you truly sit and ask the humdrum questions about what happened during the day, you don't get close to your kids. *We never would have gotten this close to our kids without Plated.*

I ask myself, "Why is everybody on some kind of diet? Why is everyone overweight? Why is everyone fat?" We are not historically an obese society, but we are today, and I believe that is because we are not sitting down to share dinner together. *I believe that if more people sat down to eat together over dinner, we'd all be healthier and happier.*

Second Course

The Plated Mission: Why a New Form of Food
Production and Distribution Is Necessary
If We Are Going to Reconnect with Our Food

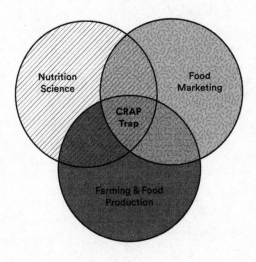

4

"City Boy Goes Country"— Farming and Food Production

One-liner: The way food is grown, produced, and manufactured in the United States is making us sick. It doesn't need to be this way.

As noted earlier, my dad's family is from Istanbul, and my mom's family is from South Dakota. In order to more fully wrap my head around how food is grown and produced in modern America, I decided to pay a visit to the ol' family farm in Dimock, South Dakota, eighty miles west of Sioux Falls, population 125.

My great-great-grandpa and namesake, Nicolaus Goddicksen, emigrated from Germany to the United States in 1878. After spending two unsuccessful years panning for gold in Colorado, some intrepid soul told him about the Homestead Act and the Dakota Territories.

The monumental Homestead Act of 1862 provided the major catalyst for the settling of the American West. The United States government encouraged the country's westward expansion by turning over vast amounts of unsettled, public land to private citizens. The government granted 160 acres of land to a homesteader at the end of five years if he lived on the land, built a house on it, and farmed it. Not only did many American families move from the East to the Great Plains, but many European immigrants also took advantage of the opportunity to at last own land for themselves.[1] Nicolaus made his way for the prairie, chasing the ever-present American dream of land and freedom.

In July of 2016, I took a few days away from the office and kids and made the sojourn from New York to South Dakota. As the plane took off from Newark Liberty International Airport, we banked hard, and I got a clean view of the Statue of Liberty and Ellis Island. Great-Great-Grandpa Nicolaus would have passed through those hallowed halls 138 years earlier. My commute to the original homestead would take me a connection in Minneapolis and a ninety-minute drive, all in about eight hours of travel time door to door. I wondered how long that same journey took Nicolaus, and what he was thinking as he ventured off to start a new life in hostile country, young, broke, and barely speaking English.

Starting our descent from my layover in Minneapolis as we crossed into South Dakota airspace, green squares stretched to the horizon like a giant's chessboard. Here and there, I spied a house, a church spire, a silo, a road, but these markers of modern man were drowned in a sea of undulating green leaves.

I got a bit lost on my way to Interstate 90 while driving out of Sioux Falls. Multiple billboards along the side of the road proclaimed, "Global Warming Is A Fact! 13,926 Scientific Papers Support Global Warming! Only 24 Did Not!" and "Evolution Is A Fact! Evolution

Proceeded All On Its Own From The Beginning! NO SUPREME BEING REQUIRED!" both prominently authored by SiouxFalls-Scientists.com. Within a few blocks of the main thoroughfare that cuts through downtown Sioux Falls, the road I was on ran directly into a cornfield, stalks as high as my waist. My mom always rhymed that corn should be "knee high by the Fourth of July," and apparently, this growing season was not falling short of the old adage.

Instead of taking the Google Maps recommended I-90, I ventured for County Road #42. As buildings gave way to houses and houses succumbed to infinite fields, I set the car on cruise control at seventy-five miles per hour and fell into a trance as the brownish-red-and-black pavement unfurled in front of me like some perpetual tongue.

The amount of corn I drove past on my eighty-mile drive to Dimock was just staggering. As I crested hills, I could see the dense junglelike leaves and the golden trestles of budding cornstalks rolling for miles in all four directions until the horizon. The occasional field of undulating green-and-brown wheat and what seemed to my untrained eye to be plots of soybeans interspersed themselves like small bit players intruding on a monologue. But it was clear that the star here was our good friend teosinte—corn.

"Farming Ain't What It Used to Be"

My time in South Dakota drove home for me that the way most commodity food is grown, produced, and manufactured in the United States today is bad for the food supply chain, bad for the environment, bad for the economy, and bad for our waistlines. The food production system is not sustainable or designed for health and happiness—and that is true for both farmers and consumers.

Farming has changed about as dramatically as an industry can change since Nicolaus Goddicksen first staked his claim in 1880.

While my family has few written records harkening back to the "good ol' days," a twentysomething-year-old Norwegian immigrant and pioneer named Ole Edvart Rølvaag homesteaded in South Dakota around the same time and went on to write the Pulitzer Prize–winning novel *Giants in the Earth*. The novel was an immediate success and is praised as one of the most powerful novels that chronicles pioneer life in America. It concentrates primarily on the hardships faced by the pioneer farmers trying to scratch out a life for themselves on the bleak and unforgiving prairie in the late nineteenth century. The book is one epic battle between man and the inhospitable Great Plains. The novel ends with the protagonist freezing to death while taking shelter against a haystack.

One evening, I sat down with my uncle Ron, a big man in his early seventies who has the cracked hands, neck, and eye corners of someone who has spent the vast majority of his life working and living outdoors. My mom's mom (my grandma) left the farm in the 1940s to go to nursing school, then Switzerland, after my grandpa was transferred there with Cargill, then Minneapolis, where my mom was born. Grandma's older sister is Ron's mom, who was born and lived on the farm until she died a few years ago. Ron wears Wrangler jeans, drives a Ford F-150, and has a predilection for fish-themed button-down work shirts and trucker hats emblazoned with the logos of different fertilizer and seed purveyors.

It is temptingly easy to overromanticize a farmer's life. After a long day in the field and doing chores in the barn, when the sun is setting and the shadows are long, this life seems less stressful and better than what most of us have become accustomed to. But the life of a twenty-first-century family farmer is far from easy.

During my time on the family farm, we talked about the neck-scorching, finger-bending, backbreaking work of tending to dozens of animals multiple times per day seven days per week when it's seventy below zero in the dead of winter and over one hundred degrees in the shade during the peak of August. A few years ago, Ron forgot to take his truck out of gear and managed to trip and fall and run over both of his own legs, and we talked about the pain he still has and the stress he feels in being unable to take even a few days off work since there's just no one else who he can rely on. Ron's wife, Dawn, and I talked about being chased out of a field by a febrile misogynistic bull. We talked about their kids leaving the farm for easier lives and never coming back. We talked about little to no retirement savings and the heartache of selling or renting your land to make ends meet.

At sunset one day, Ron spent an hour driving me around the farm and county roads that comprise the "1,300 or so" acres that he farms. For a person who lives in a two-bedroom apartment spitting distance from Manhattan, the farm felt like a truly massive amount of land, which it is—the farm is nearly twice the size of Central Park. We drove over and paid a visit to Nicolaus Goddicksen in the family cemetery, and as the sun plastered its final rays over the gravestones, we watched the deer hightail it away toward the tree line.

While in traditional real estate you might refer to square feet or maybe acres, in South Dakota farmer speak, you need a larger unit of measurement, and that is the "section." One section is one square mile, or 640 acres. As I spent time with farmers, they talked about "quarters" meaning a quarter of a section, or 160 acres. At first, I didn't understand how they could keep track of which acres were where and how much was farmed by whom, but then I realized that the entire state of South Dakota was built to simplify this process. Going from west to east, avenues go from 1st to 487th. And in the other direction, streets go from 1st in the north to 335th Street in the south, where Nebraska, Iowa, and South Dakota collide along the Missouri River.

My relatives farm more than a full section that encompasses fields between 268th and 269th Streets and 399th and 400th Avenues. One morning, I got up with the sunrise and ran the four miles around the section on the dirt roads that frame the perimeter of the corn and soy fields. I was greeted by a herd of black cattle who stared at me with curiosity and then in one mass turned their hides on me and thundered away to the opposite end of the field.

On the way to the field one day, we turned a corner, and Ron whistled. "Whoa, look at that corn! Put an inch of rain on top of that and it would be the cat's meow!" He cooed this admiringly, as if he were an adolescent boy marveling at the older girl back from college working as a lifeguard at the local public pool. Corn was in-extricably tied to farming, and farming was life. It was beautiful, it was hard, sometimes it sucked, sometimes it was glorious. And the truth was in the details.

Ron had done this job since he was in elementary school. I asked him why, at seventy years old, he was still at it. He took a moment to think, and then he said, "I just love it, you know. I love the sun-rise and the sunset. When you're out here a part of this world every day, it's magical, you know. I would probably just be doing the same thing with myself if I went and retired."

I asked Ron what's the hardest part of farming.

"Oh, it must be the unpredictability," he responded. "I mean, the good Lord gives and he takes, you know. But you're at the mercy of the weather. And that can be tough some years. This year is ques-tionable if we'll make any money. It all depends on yield per acre and price on the board in Chicago. If you don't own your own land, you're probably not gonna make any money these days."

Family farming is at its core a form of family-owned business, where the fundamental asset is the land, the customer is the local grain elevator that pays at Chicago market rates, the merchandise is the seeds produced, and the costs are the inputs to make a harvest. Each of these guys (and all the farmers I met were guys) had to keep a running profit-and-loss statement in his head at all times. Ron walked me through some of his numbers, and that's when it all clicked for me:

These guys live on a corn leaf's edge of razor-thin margins. They own their land, but they are indentured to it, the same way an immigrant Dunkin' Donuts franchisee has the rights to his store but has to work twenty hours a day, seven days a week, just to break even.

If the rain is delayed by three weeks; if storms dropping golf ball–sized hail roll through; if temperatures stay north of ninety for too long; if another part of the Midwest experiences a bumper crop that drives down the price per bushel that is determined in Chicago—any one of these factors could wipe out a year of work and investment.

Coming from my world, where you control for all risks by using data and technology, it was shocking to fully comprehend that something as fickle and uncontrollable as the weather could destroy your entire business model in a matter of minutes.

Federal crop insurance is there to help. For $8 per acre, Ron can insure his crop up to $450 in revenue per acre. But crop insurance has become a very unnatural thing and poses a philosophical quandary for farmers like Uncle Ron, who is socially and fiscally conservative, and for whom the idea of taking government "handouts" is anathema to his way of life. This insurance should cost five times as much or more, but the Farm Service Agency and other federal programs help subsidize the costs and make it possible for farmers like Ron to buy insurance and stay in business.

This struck me as the equivalent of Plated being supported through federally regulated shipping discounts—"Oh, FedEx is too expensive for your current business model? Well, don't worry about that; let Uncle Sam and the taxpayers help you make your business model profitable." This seemed totally bizarre to me— farms are not run as private-public partnerships or nonprofit offshoots of the government. If a business doesn't make a profit on its own merits and needs significant support from the government just to limp along from year to year, can you still even consider it to be a business?

I was driving in a semi down a dusty road to meet Ron at the combine. I asked his nephew Eric, who is just a few years older than I am with two kids, "Do you ever think about not farming?"

"Every day." He laughed. Then he turned more serious. "Especially recently. It's just so lopsided, you know."

I asked what he meant.

"Well, it's just so damn hard to make any money. Someone else is always making the money, but us farmers? We get nothing. What I told my nephew who is now in the air force is that he should stay in for twenty years, then once he's got his pension and his insurance taken care of, he should come back and farm and have fun with it. But this ain't much fun without a cushion to fall back on. Farming ain't what it used to be."

I very easily could have been Eric in another iteration of my life. I was one generation removed from the farm, but I lived in a completely different universe.

Subsidies for Corn and Soy Have Dramatically Altered American Food Production

One afternoon, I decided to escape the sun and fields and take a mini–road trip to "town"—also known as Mitchell, South Dakota, population 15,256, home to the World's Only Corn Palace. The "Palace" is a sports arena and theater whose exterior is entirely wrapped in murals that are made from different parts of the corn plant. The exterior corn murals are replaced and redesigned each year with a new theme—when I visited, the theme was "Rock of Ages" and featured corn kernel thirty-foot-high portraits of Elvis and Willie Nelson. In the late 1800s, a number of cities on the Great Plains constructed "crop palaces" (also known as "grain palaces") to promote themselves and their products, such as the original Mitchell Corn Palace, which "was built in 1892 to showcase the rich soil of South Dakota and encourage people to settle in the area."[2] By this time, Nicolaus had already been homesteading the farm, growing and selling corn for over a decade.

Corn is to this part of the world what oil is to Texas, what money is to New York, and what technology is to Silicon Valley. It is the lifeblood, and it carries a history and culture that is inseparable from the land and the people. The local middle school and high school sports teams are not the Tigers or the Pirates or the Lions but the Kernels. The local news radio station is 1490 KORN. The lampposts on Main Street are emblazoned with corncobs.

By the time I got back to the farm, a fifteen-mile drive due south from Mitchell, it was time for dinner. It was still ninety degrees outside, and after driving with the windows down across dirt and gravel roads, I was dusty and parched. Dawn met me at the door and said, "You look like you could use a drink!"

She poured me a brimming frozen stein full of what looked like a Michelada. It was cold and crisp and perfect. What do you call this thing?

Ron sauntered in from his office. "Well, I call it tomato beer. It's just beer and juice from tomatoes that we raised in the garden." After Ron and Dawn sold off their dairy herd, Ron took up gardening as a hobby, and they now kept a basketball court–sized plot a stone's throw from their kitchen. That night for dinner, we had mashed red russet garlic potatoes that Ron and I pulled directly from the soil, sweet corn, and a huge slab of rib eye steak that Ron did on the grill.

The steak dissolved like meaty ice cream between saliva-spawning chomps. I asked, mostly jokingly, if Ron had killed the cow himself, and he responded, "Sort of." The 1,700-pound Angus that furnished our dinner had been raised by Danny, Ron's brother-in-law. Ron paid Danny $1.70 per pound for four hundred pounds of meat, about a quarter of the animal. Ron was peeved because the price subsequently dropped to below $1.20. An additional dollar of "processing fees" brought the total price per pound to around $3.00.

In my world, *processing fees* refers to how much our credit card vendors take when we charge a customer for their order. In Ron's world, it was slaughtering, skinning, cutting, and packaging to go from cow to kitchen. The cow was antibiotic-free, grass fed, grain finished, and processed just a few miles from where we were savoring the beast's contribution to this world. And that three-dollar one-pound rib eye was probably the best steak I ever had.

But it made me wonder, what does it say about our country and the way we raise our food that a pound of meat of this quality could cost less than a gallon of gas? Is this a hallmark of our food production and distribution system being impressively broken, bountiful, or both?

Farm subsidies have had a profound effect on how American food is grown, produced, and distributed. Traditionally, the American government tended to stay out of the farm business and the business of farmers. It takes a very strong-willed, independent person to be a farmer, and those personality traits tend to mix with federal supervision like oil with water. In the 1930s, despite the fact that food prices were at an all-time low, Americans still couldn't afford food, and the food surpluses and simultaneous farm crisis persisted to the point that the federal government decided to get involved.

Farm subsidies, quotas, and tariffs have profoundly affected agricultural production and, ultimately, the American diet. Even after the farm crises of the Great Depression and Dust Bowl concluded, many subsidies remained.

Corn, the most prolific crop in America, is one example. Federal subsidies of corn are among the highest of any commodity, amounting to $30 billion between 1996 and 2001. A third of total farm payments made by the government go toward corn.[3] These subsidies are used to reduce the cost of production, which result in a flooding of the market with artificially cheap products that are stuffed full of corn.

The unholy alliance between Big Food and lobbyists who aid in the proliferation of corn and soy subsidies is directly responsible for producing the unhealthful foods that define our Flawed American Diet. Over the last fifty years, farm policy has focused on increasing subsidies for commodities, primarily corn and soybeans. This has led to an oversupply that has in turn made it harder and harder for farmers to make a profit, leading to a greater emphasis on maximizing yield and a growing reliance on government subsidy payments. This vicious flywheel hurts the farmer, hurts the planet, and hurts us as consumers.

Simultaneously, smaller farms were purchased by big conglomerate farm holding companies that could more easily operationalize and profit from large-volume commodity sales. Large corporations that purchased the cheap grain profited, and agriculture in the United States became an increasingly industrial sector. As Big Food grew bigger, family-owned businesses found it harder and harder to compete.

The glut of cheap corn and soybeans has directly and negatively influenced how we as a society produce our food. Factory farm animals that are raised on grain and soy are significantly cheaper to produce, which leads to more profits. These profits are reinvested in achieving greater scale, in turn generating even more profits, and even larger factory farms. Despite significant scale and profit advantages, subsidies continue to distort the market for corn and soy.

Although some subsidy programs are intended to provide a safety net for small farmers in cases of low production or poor profitability due to weather, market price variations, and other factors, most farmers in the United States do not benefit from subsidies. Various restrictions often prevent small farmers from enrolling in subsidy programs and collecting payments. None of the family farmers that I met received direct payouts for their grain production. Between 1995 and 2009, 10 percent of farmers received 74 percent of farm subsidies, and 62 percent of U.S. farmers did not collect any subsidies.[4]

From Farm to Factory

At dinner, I asked Ron if we were eating the same corn that he grows in the fields. "Oh no." He guffawed. "This is the nursery variety, not the Roundup type—I don't want to eat that stuff." I thought that was a strange comment, since he grows hundreds of acres of corn but paradoxically doesn't eat any of it, and I asked what he meant by Roundup.

Since the 1990s, the Monsanto Company has been developing and selling "Roundup Ready Corn" seeds. Roundup Ready plants are genetically engineered to be resistant to Monsanto's herbicide Roundup. Farmers that plant Roundup Ready seeds must use the Roundup herbicide to prevent weeds from growing in their fields. The products, when used in tandem, work remarkably well. Over the last thirty years, Ron has been able to double his corn yield per acre by introducing the Roundup product suite to his cornfields. This magnitude of leap in efficiency is a true marvel of modern technology.

But Ron cautioned against unbridled optimism. He concluded, "I don't know exactly what the Roundup spray and seeds are doing to my land, but my dad always used to say if you think things are too good to be true, they probably are. And I imagine that's what we are going to be saying about Roundup ten to fifteen years from now."

Farmers by nature are concerned about the future. This is rooted not only in the seasonal cycles of growing but also in the fundamental uncertainty of agriculture. Farmers have historically been at the mercy of droughts, floods, and other "acts of God." Bad years were bound to come, and as a consequence, since the start of the Agricultural Revolution, the future became a farmer's obsession. Where farmers depend on rain to water their fields, like South Dakota, this means that each morning brings prayers and hopeful glances at the horizon. *Is that a storm coming? Will there be enough water for all my crops? Is that hail, and is it going to destroy the corn?*

The stress of farming formed the foundation of modern society. Throughout history, farmers rarely realized the future financial security they worked so diligently to achieve in the present. People and processes were always emerging to deprive farmers of their surplus food, leaving them scratching by with subsistence. Food surpluses were forfeited for the ruling elite, and this powered governments, armies, entertainment, and innovation.

Until the twentieth century, more than 90 percent of the world was farmers. The extra food they produced fed the elite minority, folks like politicians, generals, priests, and artists. As one historian wrote, "History is something that very few people have been doing while everyone else was plowing fields and carrying water buckets."[5]

The largest accomplishment of modern society is that food is much more widely distributed and that most Americans are no longer farmers. I'm not degrading farming or farmers but admiring technology's ability to improve productivity and well-being. Yields and efficiency on everything from farm tools to fertilizers to crops have improved dramatically. This has allowed tens of millions of Americans to break free from the yoke of indentured servitude to the land. In 1900, around 41 percent of America's labor force worked on a farm. Today, the proportion is below 2 percent. But because of technology, the shrinking proportion of Americans working as farmers is still able to feed the vast urban majority—and more.

Not Sustainable or Designed
for Health and Happiness

Agriculture is now a $7.8 trillion worldwide market, but despite this enormous size, with current farming technology, in a few decades, we will be unable to feed our country—and the world.

As the global population races toward ten billion, the current level of food production will have to increase by 70 percent in order to adequately feed everyone.[6] We'll have to do it as climate change rewrites the weather rules around the globe—and as ever more of that population achieves middle-class status and wants to eat accordingly.

Depending on where they live, farmers will increasingly wrestle with either intense rainfall or ongoing drought and the insects and diseases that come with them. The Intergovernmental Panel on Climate Change concludes that changes in climate are already slowing the average growth rate for crop yields by up to 2.5 percent per decade globally. And in some parts of the world, the urgency has already reached a fever pitch. "It's going to require an incredible leap in productivity," says former U.S. secretary of agriculture Tom Vilsack. Even America, the breadbasket for the world, will have trouble keeping pace. During Vilsack's lifetime, the United States increased production by 170 percent on 26 percent less farmland. "More advanced agriculture economies aren't going to be able to make that kind of leap in the next twenty-five years," he says.[7]

Unless something big changes.

Thirty to forty percent of all perishable food is thrown away in the United States every year—that's the equivalent of hundreds of billions of dollars in food waste annually. If we could reduce this to Plated's food-waste number, this initiative alone would get us halfway to the goal of feeding the world as the population balloons to ten billion by 2050. But we'll need more than just waste reduction.

We are most likely not going to create more farmland. Consequently, the growth in food production must come from more efficiency and higher yields. Agriculture has undergone yield-enhancing shifts in the past, including the introduction of new crop varieties and agricultural chemicals in the green revolution of the 1950s and 1960s. Yet yields of important crops have now stopped rising in many places, a phenomenon called yield plateauing. To go beyond these plateaus will require better technology.[8]

No part of solving this problem is going to be easy. Farmers tend to fear change, since the downside of losing an entire harvest rarely outweighs the upside of experimentation. Yet if technological solutions play out as many—including me—hope, a technology-driven change in food production may be close at hand.

Silicon Valley Meets Silicon Prairie

In December 2015, a Virginian farmer named David Hula won the National Corn Growers Association's annual yield contest by squeezing 532 bushels of corn out of a single acre—a world record that trounced the 2015 U.S. national average by a factor of more than three.[9]

Hula had to get everything perfect to reach that prize-winning yield: planting his rows the right distance apart, treating the soil with the precise microbes needed to keep it healthy, applying the ideal amount of nitrogen fertilizer at the ideal moment. Farmers make some forty decisions like these each season—decisions that were once made largely by tradition and training but that are now reached increasingly with the help of data.

"Precision farming" (using data to optimize agricultural output) has begun to revolutionize food production. One way to view farming is as calculus. A farmer must constantly juggle a large set of variables—the weather, the cost of fertilizer, seed selection, threats to crops from pests, and the price that he will get when he harvests and sells. If he does the math correctly, or if it is done on his behalf by machines, he will optimize his yield and maximize his profit. In the world of miniscule margins, where a few dollars per acre can make the difference between profitability and bankruptcy, this optimization is essential. Precision farming's success will be enabled through the adoption of sensors, software, digital connectivity, and most importantly, data.

On my way back to New York, I stopped in Sioux Falls at Farmers Business Network (FBN) to see what the future of farming looks like. After working at Google for several years, Charles Baron, one of my college roommates, saw an opportunity to harness data and technology to improve farmers' lives, and he started FBN. I met up with Andy Cahoy, who runs the Midwest headquarters of FBN in a nondescript, single-story office next to a dialysis center on the outskirts of Sioux Falls.

Andy looks like a lot of the guys who went through infantry training with me: tall, lean, and reserved with a close-cropped shock of wheat-blond hair that hadn't seen an army razor in a few years. He grew up in South Dakota, went to West Point, deployed to Afghanistan as an infantry officer, and recently completed his MBA at Stanford.

We talked about missing military life, his deployment to Afghanistan, and his decision to turn down Google to return to South Dakota to help build FBN. He was taciturn at first, but when we started talking about FBN, his excitement was palpable. "Farms these days are generating tons of data! The changes that have happened in the last ten years are unbelievable! You've got planting data, seed treatments, pest information, chemical applications, harvest data—the challenge for farmers has always been 'What do we do with all this data?'"

Farmers take enormous amounts of risk every year in making their decisions. Prior to FBN, the best way for farmers to understand how they were performing was for them to ask their fertilizer and seed dealers. There are pretty obvious perverse incentives to asking a salesman about your performance—it's like asking the car dealer if you should upgrade to the luxury model.

FBN has built an independent, unbiased farmer-to-farmer network. They connect dozens of pieces of farm data from millions of acres of land across thousands of member farmers all over the United States and use that data to help farmers find actionable insights on their operations—ways that they can cut costs, save money, and increase yield through transparency. The idea is that there is power in numbers, and the value doesn't just come from yourself—the value is looking anonymously at what farmers are doing around you and seeing how you may be able to implement those same practices to be successful on your farm.

Big Data is essential to the business model.[10] "The idea here is kind of like money ball for farming," Andy explains. Farming is a game of statistics that farmers unwittingly play every day. By looking at the average yields and what the data tells you, there are a lot of powerful decisions that you can make based on that information that farmers weren't able to make before. They would, and still do, go off and plant one- or two-acre test-plotted corn, and say, "Okay, that test plot yielded this many bushels per acre, so I think I can get that everywhere." But the reality is that data like that is highly flawed, and it's not relevant, real-world information. FBN has a large network and database of real-world performance information, thousands of seed varieties, based on real-world conditions in real-world soil types that are highly relevant to farmers in each growing area.

"If I had one wish for farming today," Andy tells me, "it would be to make it more transparent. Farming just has so many barriers today. It's an oligopoly; access to farmers is completely controlled by five or six big-name companies. In other industries and eras, this kind of behavior is illegal. It's like monopolistic behavior that happens all over America, and these local communities and people suffer because there is just no access to information."

The problem runs deep. Farmers work with sales agronomists, someone who knows about agronomy—but, oh, by the way, he's also trying to sell them chemicals. So there are conflicts of interest everywhere in the industry. It's hard to find independent, nonbiased advice, to the point where it is hard to break that barrier. The sales agronomist that the farmer is working with will try to convince the farmer not to sign up for FBN because it obviates the need for what services that particular agronomist offers and competes with the price of the chemicals he is trying to sell.

Andy argues that the level of transparency needs to improve because today it hurts the farmer. "The industry is definitely ripe for disruption, and that's what I'm really excited about," he says. FBN wants to break those barriers and make the industry function like any other industry does in the twenty-first century. Farmers should know what they need to pay and what a fair price is for the enormous costs that are going into every planting and harvest season.

Some folks I talked to make the analogy of FBN being the Amazon.com of agriculture. I asked Andy what he thought about that. "I think that would be awesome!"

Technology is the future of farming and food more broadly. The renowned venture capitalist Marc Andreessen famously said that technology is eating the world. In this case, the world is starting to eat more and more technology—or at least its by-products.

At Plated, we are proud to plant a flag and paint a vision of what the future of food will look like. The same transformations toward transparency and optimization have happened in countless industries over the last twenty years—online shopping, airline tickets, home buying, personal finance, media—but food is the final frontier. One key part of our future vision is leveraging technology to improve how food is produced.

After my trip to South Dakota, I was feeling optimistic. There is certainly a lot of hard work ahead, and there are many entrenched interests who conspire against small businesses, our health, and the environment. But it seems increasingly apparent that the problems associated with traditional farming are potentially solvable with technology and bit of grit and gumption. Unfortunately, the next step in the food supply chain is significantly more complicated.

5

The CRAP Trap

L et's turn to the impact farm subsidies have on what we eat. Most farm subsidies go to corn, wheat, cotton, and soybean production—fruits and vegetables are largely left out. Fruits, vegetables, nuts, and legumes for human consumption receive only about 2 percent of all subsidies, although these foods should constitute the majority of Americans' daily food consumption. If we ask how agricultural support programs affect consumption (and thus health), we need to look at their impact on price and food availability. The vast majority of crop subsidies directly or indirectly support the production of the least healthful foods.

This conflict between health and agricultural policies was highlighted by the President's Cancer Panel in a recent report:

Efforts to halt and reverse current obesity trends are unlikely to succeed without the participation and collaboration of governments, non-governmental organizations, industry, educators, and individuals. For example, current agricultural and public health policy is not coordinated—we heavily subsidize the growth of

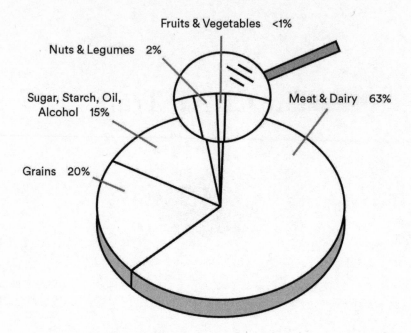

foods (e.g., corn, soy) that in their processed forms (e.g., high-fructose corn syrup, hydrogenated corn and soybean oils, grain-fed cattle) are known contributors to obesity and associated chronic diseases, including cancer.[1]

There is little question that abundant, low-cost commodity inputs distort the market for unsubsidized products and give a competitive advantage to unhealthful foods like refined fats and corn-based sweeteners. The federal government also ensures against risks of production with subsidized crop insurance that is not available for nuts, legumes, fruits, and veggies.[2] Producers who might grow fruits and vegetables, like my family in South Dakota, have a strong disincentive to do so.

To sum up what we've learned in the last few paragraphs: High-quality, nutritious food is expensive, and low-quality, unhealthy food is cheap due in large part to the pervasiveness of subsidies for commodity crops like corn and soy.

Why Is CRAP Such Crap?

One afternoon, Uncle Ron and I drove a semitruck filled with freshly harvested winter wheat to the local grain elevator. From the back of the truck, a high-powered vacuum sucked the thousands of pounds of grain up into storage silos. Twice per week, a train from BNSF pulls up to the elevator and fills twenty-six boxcars with thousands of tons of grain. If the grain in question were corn, the train would haul its load to a manufacturing facility like the Clinton Corn Processing Company, the corporation that first discovered and started marketing high-fructose corn syrup in the early 1970s.

HFCS has two interrelated advantages over other natural and artificial sweeteners. First, it is easier to process and handle than table sugar, so it can be shipped around the country and world. And second, due to the rampant American corn subsidies discussed earlier, it is significantly less expensive than other sources of sweet.

The consumption of HFCS increased over 1,000 percent between 1970 and 1990, far exceeding the changes in intake of any other food or food group. HFCS now represents more than 40 percent of caloric sweeteners added to foods and beverages and is essentially the sole caloric sweetener in soft drinks in the United

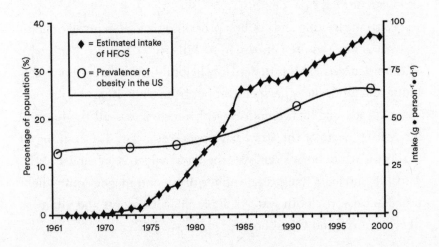

States.[3] There is no question that HFCS has had a fiftyfold growth in annual per capita consumption and that this occurred in lockstep with the four-decade obesity epidemic in America (see the preceding graph). There is now research to support that a marked increase in the use of HFCS preceded the obesity epidemic and may be an important contributor to the obesity epidemic in the United States and around the world.[4]

While Big Food insiders will argue that this is correlation and not causation, it should certainly raise some eyebrows and questions.

The Stripping of Nutrition and Joy

There are two main reasons why chemically processed foods are bad for us. We eat food because it gives us joy and it gives us nutrition. But when food is hyperprocessed, both the joy and the nutrition are stripped out.

What's left over is food in name only. From both a production and nutrient perspective, our ancestors wouldn't recognize the ingredients or the processes required to make riskily altered provisions. It is clean, it is easy, it is stable—but CRAP is dead food, and as any good zombie aficionado can appreciate, hanging out with the dead can be very bad for you.

Extreme heating and cooling processes that often involve chemical baths are required in order to kill bacteria and other active microorganisms. This is undeniably helpful from a consistency, stability, and food-safety perspective, but from a nutrition and joy perspective, it's like high school English censorship—all the fun and interesting parts of the story have been removed. The refining of grains for white breads removes the husk, which stores most of the valuable nutrients like protein, fiber, iron, and magnesium. These processes destroy both water-soluble micronutrients and vitamins like vitamin B and C and hosts of good bacteria.

As we are still in the predawn equivalent of gut microbiome research, we don't yet fully understand the role and significance of microbes in our diet and on our health and psychology, but it may be possible to cultivate a healthier community of bacteria on and inside us by eating more "dirty foods"—foods that haven't been processed literally to death.

It comes down to this: Riskily altered food is missing nutrient density. If you're primarily eating riskily altered food, then you're not getting the nutrients that your body needs to survive and thrive. So either you're not getting these nutrients, which is bad for your general health, or you need to eat many more calories in order to get them, and you overconsume and get fat. On the other hand, if you're consuming "nutrient dense" foods (fresh foods that aren't processed), then you can get all the nutrients you need with many fewer calories.

Ultimately, as shelf stability is enhanced, nutrients are removed, and so are the flavors. In order to replace those missing flavors, various forms of low-nutrient fillers are added back.

Flavors and Fillers:
The Sweet, the Fat, and the Ugly

The two most potent riskily altered provisions in the Big Food arsenal are sweeteners and fat. However, the Big Food players themselves are stuck in the CRAP Trap. As Pulitzer Prize–winning investigative journalist Michael Moss reports, "It had taken me three and a half years of prying into the food industry's operations to come to terms with the full range of institutional forces that compel even the best companies to churn out foods that undermine a healthy diet." Despite their best efforts, Big Food's unrelenting need to create the most taste for the lowest possible cost has pulled it back again and again to these two deeply addictive bullets.[5]

The Sweet

The World Health Organization has recommended that people limit their consumption of added sugars to 10 percent of calories, but experts say that typical consumption of empty calories in the United States is nearly twice that level. How did sweeteners become such an omnipresent part of the way America eats?[6]

There are special receptors for sweetness in every one of the mouth's ten thousand taste buds, and they are all hooked up, one way or another, to the parts of the brain known as the pleasure zones, where we get rewarded for stoking our bodies with energy. Scientists are now finding taste receptors that light up for sugar all the way down our esophagus to our stomach and pancreas, and they appear to be intricately tied to our appetites.[7]

Big Food deploys armies of scientists who specialize in the senses, and the companies use their knowledge to put sweeteners to work for them in countless ways. Sugar not only makes the taste of otherwise bland food and drink irresistible; the industry has learned that it can also be used to pull off a string of manufacturing miracles, from fish sticks that fry up bigger and browner to yogurt with a six-month shelf life. All of this has made sweeteners a go-to ingredient in processed foods. On average, as Americans, we consume seventy-one pounds of caloric sweeteners each year. That's twenty-two teaspoons of sweet per person per day.[8]

As a man much wiser than I once said, and I paraphrase, "It's sort of like if you drink alcohol really fast, you get drunk really fast." This is what happens when we rapidly overconsume refined sweeteners. We are programmed to like highly refined sweets because they bring us immediate pleasure. Again, think back to our hunter-gatherer ancestors stumbling across a tree bulging with fruit in the jungle. When you are starving and uncertain when and where your next meal will come, it makes sense to gorge on high-calorie sources of nutrition when they are available. When your body is adapted to operating in a low-sugar environment, these excess calories get converted into adipose tissue that can be called upon for energy when the next lion attacks.

But in the modern age of overabundance and overconsumption, obviously there are consequences to bingeing. When you break down sugar quickly, your body gets flooded with more glucose than it can handle, which triggers an insulin response to suck the sugar out of the bloodstream, which leads to an eventual glucose crash, which leads to the body craving more sugar. It is a vicious cycle.

As a consequence, the overconsumption of sugar has increasingly been tied to the obesity epidemic. Food processing worked miracles in the United States starting after World War II, enabling Big Food to supply hundreds of millions of people with unprecedented levels of calories—starvation was heading the way of the dodo.

Success bred success, and Big Food exported its low-cost, high-calorie taste paradigm around the world. Overeating is now a global issue. In China, for the first time in history, the overnourished now outnumber the malnourished. In France, where obesity has climbed from 8.5 percent to 14.5 percent since 1997, Nestlé has been enjoying great success in selling the Jenny Craig weight-loss program to the same French folk who once sneered at Americans' proclivity to jump from one diet fad to another. Mexico's obesity rate has tripled in the past three decades, leading to worries that it now has the fattest kids in the world.[9]

The United States, however, remains the most obese country in human history. And where the rates of obesity appear to be reaching a plateau among adults at 35 percent, they are still climbing among the group that is the most vulnerable to the food industry's products: children. The most recent data shows that obesity among kids aged six to eleven jumped from 15 to 20 percent.

Sugar not only sweetens, it also helps to reduce costs. By replacing more expensive (and nutritious) ingredients like tomatoes in ketchup, sweeteners add bulk, texture, and allure while improving the bottom line. This is a win-win for Big Food, but a big fat doughnut for our health and, ultimately, our happiness as consumers.

The Fat

Fat is not part of our official roster of primary tastes, which currently consists of just five members: sweet, salty, sour, bitter, and a more recent addition known as umami, which is a meaty, savory taste derived from an amino acid called glutamate. As a consequence, sometimes it is hard to determine if fat has been added to foods at all.

Because of fat's remarkable powers, Big Food relies on it like no other component. Fat turns sad chips into crunchy marvels, parched breads into silky loaves, drab meat into savory lunch. Like sugar, some types of fat furnish processed foods with one of their most fundamental requirements: the capacity to sit on the grocery store shelf for months or years at a time. Fat also gives cookies more bulk and a firmer texture. It substitutes for water in lending tenderness and mouthfeel to crackers. It lessens the rubbery texture in hot dogs, deepens their color, keeps them from sticking to the grill, and, as an added bonus, saves Big Food money, since the fattier trimmings of meat they use in making hot dogs cost less to buy than the leaner cuts.[10]

Fat has a final trait, however, that makes it even more essential than sugar in processed foods. The fat bullet doesn't blast away at our mouths like sweet does; it's more CIA than Marine Corps infantry. As Michael Moss wrote, "If sugar is the methamphetamine of processed food ingredients, with its high-speed, blunt assault on our brains, then fat is the opiate, a smooth operator whose effects are less obvious but no less powerful."[11]

The increased prevalence of soybean oil usage and consumption is a prime example of this. The most commonly consumed vegeta-

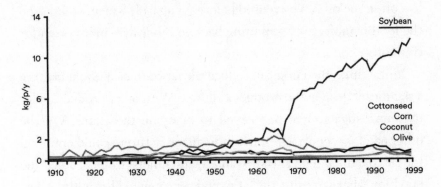

ble oil in the United States is soybean oil. Most people don't realize they're eating soybean oil at all, let alone hundreds of calories per day from the second–most heavily subsidized American crop (behind corn). Most of these surreptitious calories come from riskily altered foods, which often have soybean oil added to them because it is cheap and adds good texture and mouthfeel.

Soybean oil consumption increased over a thousandfold over the course of the twentieth century. We talk about olive oil all the time, but the chart above captures the full fat story. At the end of the twentieth century, soybean oil accounted for 7 percent of all calories consumed in the United States. It's pretty insane for any food to account for that high of a percentage of caloric consumption.[12]

Reducing the amount of fat in its products is not easy for Big Food. They can't allow this to diminish the taste or texture, or they will lose sales. Nor can they let a reduction in fat cause their production costs to rise too high, or they will lose profits.

The most important variable is how much more money customers are willing to spend for a better product. For example, fiddling with the fat used for frying has serious implications for the bottom line of food manufacturers. It's relatively easy to cut down on the fat in fried foods. All you have to do is turn up the temperature of the oil being used for frying. But the higher the temperature, the less often the oil can be reused before going bad, which would send the food manufacturers running back to oil dealers more often for fresh oil.

Sometimes Big Food can reduce the fat content without causing a significant drop in the product's allure.[13] With other products, adding more sugar might be needed to maintain the allure. On the other hand, as reported, "these same manufacturers could crank up the fat content as high as they wanted, and unless people studied the nutrition label carefully, the fat would get eaten in bliss without setting off any alarms in the body's system that help regulate our weight by telling us we are eating too much."[14]

Why Can't Big Food Kick Its Bad Habit?

The Big Food cardinal rule is that nutritional improvements can't come at the cost of less mouthfeel, flavor, and general appeal. These are the factors that keep consumers coming back, and if these factors are diminished, profits take a beating. Again, the folks that run the biggest food companies are not evil—they are just caught in a trap of their own making, where they can't maintain their profitability and change their products fast enough. Big Food's riskily altered offerings are increasingly out of sync with what consumers want, but profits must be preserved ahead of meaningful product improvements. The fundamental problem is that Big Food built a business model and food system that no longer works. And that is why Plated is building a new and better system for delivering fresh food from the ground up.

More and more consumers have come to focus on fat and sweeteners, whether out of concern for obesity and heart disease or simply a desire to eat food that is less processed and more real. Elected officials, from President Obama to New York City mayor Michael Bloomberg, have also elevated their criticism of riskily altered foods.

The response from Big Food has been to give consumers more of a choice by turning out "healthier" versions of their traditional products. The further they go down this path, however, the harder they bump up against two stark realities of the industrial food model they created.

Profits Don't Need to Come at the Expense of Sustainability and Transparency

Look, I get it. At Plated, we run a for-profit company, and we're proud of it. A *for-profit company* is exactly that: *for profit*. As I learned in Indonesia running our microfinance institution, the only way to truly scale and have massive impact is to make a profit—otherwise, you will always be beholden to donors. But that doesn't mean the profit motive should replace doing what's best for people.

At Plated, our First Core Belief is: *Transparency and control over personal and planetary health are essential*. In many businesses, but especially in the food industry, there has traditionally been little to no transparency. Technology and data are essential to our new and better model.

Picture of an Evolved Eater

Sally Robling is Plated's chairman. She joined us in 2014 and has been instrumental in helping Josh and me structure our business and our board of directors for scale.

I began my career in 1982 working on Shake 'n Bake at the company that ultimately became Kraft. I spent the next eighteen years at Kraft and Campbell in marketing and sales, working on some of the most iconic American food brands, including Jell-O and Campbell's, and with the largest food retailers. I returned to food in 2008, Pinnacle Foods, where I led the $1 billion Birds Eye Division through the company's IPO.

I left Pinnacle, and Big Food, after Pinnacle's successful 2013 IPO. My intent was to work with entrepreneurs who understood how much food had to change and who were applying new thinking and technologies to drive the change. I'd spent much of my career on dinner and trying to help consumers fit a home-cooked meal into their busy and fragmented lives at least a couple of times a week.

I sought Nick and Josh out because I knew they were trying to solve a big problem. If Plated worked, its customers could make a really good dinner at home on any night. The behavior was high value and frequent, so the addressable market was very large. Then I met Nick and Josh, and I was compelled by their passion, pragmatism, and grit. I believed that they could go the distance and that I could add valuable perspective and experience. As I dug deeper, I realized that this was not just about dinner but about building a new, radically more efficient food supply chain. At that point, while having no real idea of how hard this would be, I was in—with an investment in money and, more importantly, my time.

What makes Plated work, its core competency, is found in the middle of a Venn diagram that integrates proprietary big data, a highly flexible, distributed supply chain, with a consumer-centric brand built on the conviction that food is joy to be celebrated and that thoughtful design should permeate everything. Lots of companies do one, maybe two—but few do all three—and that is why Plated delivers an exceptional, tailored consumer experience with radical efficiency.

It's superior to other food models because it starts from the consumers and how they live now, not an extant infrastructure, and because, while it's got deep culinary and food fulfillment expertise, it's not a food company—but this very new hybrid of food, tech, and an experiential, creative brand. Truly right brain / left brain.

Data binds together culinary artistry and consumer desires to yield an evolving, increasingly personalized and delightful consumer experience. I was deeply concerned that when the creative culinary process was married to the big data emerging from consumer behavior, it would be a drag on the chefs and their creative process and could drive them to dull and uniform menus. I was wrong. The marriage of data and culinary skill has had just the opposite effect. It's been a dramatic and powerful accelerant to the chefs' creativity in the service of providing our consumers tailored, and deeply satisfying, menus and experiences.

The data drives a personalized, continuously improving customer experience and radically more efficient supply chain. In conventional food systems (manufacturer to retailer to consumer), the data travels through multiple handoffs and the actual consumer eating experience is never captured, so the data signals are weak. In contrast, Plated data comes directly from the consumer and is both backward and forward looking, so the signals are powerful and immediate. That means that, even with and because of the consumer experience of flexibility and personalization, the food-waste levels in production and at home are very low and multiples less than in a conventional food supply chain. The efficiency of food use has profound benefits to the consumer, Plated, and, over time, the planet.

6

The Cacophony of Confusion

One-liner: The average American citizen still doesn't know what or how he or she should be eating. We will walk through the cacophony of confusion that is created through modern food marketing and federal nutrition guidelines.

Every day, we are inundated with information, yet the average American citizen still doesn't know what or how he or she should be eating.

So what *should* we be eating? And why? The deeper I dug into that question, the more complicated the answer became. And when things get complicated, we often fail.

If you've read any food books, blogs, or articles lately—especially ones that attempt to posit new ideas about what we should be eating—you may have smelled some controversy brewing. Food is a hot topic, and there is plenty of literature by medical doctors and investigative journalists, many of whom have penned more than one bestseller on the subject. The good news is there has never been so much information in the market dealing with food and nutrition.

The bad news is the authors rarely agree with one another, and it's hard to know which guidance to follow.

One thing they all seem to agree on is that Big Food continues to support and uphold the model it created. You'd be hard-pressed to find one of these authors who *doesn't* think the big multinational corporations and fast-food behemoths are fouling up our pantries and our arteries. Food authors and activists also all seem to agree that the American diet is significantly flawed. The proof is in the pudding, in the sense that "the pudding" includes more than seventy-eight million obese Americans and countless others struggling with health issues springing from a diet laden with riskily altered food.

But beyond a basic agreement on the perpetrators, there's quite a bit of controversy on what exactly we ought to do about it. As I started to read all the popular food books by Michael Pollan, Gary Taubes, Nina Teicholz, Michael Moss, Marion Nestle, William Davis, and many others, just to know what I should do to change my diet, I also began to plumb just how deeply Big Food has influenced our decision making.

Do you think you understand why you choose to buy and eat certain foods?

If you answered, "Yes!" then I congratulate you, because you have the same collective knowledge as the thousand-plus food scientists who have been working at the world's largest food companies studying this exact question, all day, every day, for the last sixty years.

Choosing food is about much more than calories or nutrition content. Humans pick food and food products based on how we expect them to taste and feel in our mouths, not to mention the sig-

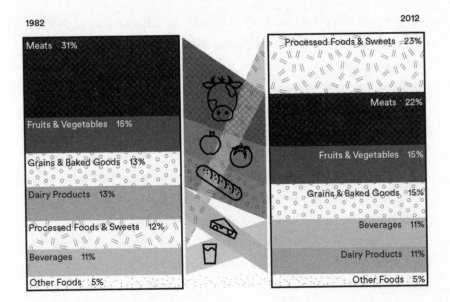

1982

Meats   31%

Fruits & Vegetables   15%

Grains & Baked Goods   13%

Dairy Products   13%

Processed Foods & Sweets   12%

Beverages   11%

Other Foods   5%

2012

Processed Foods & Sweets   23%

Meats   22%

Fruits & Vegetables   15%

Grains & Baked Goods   15%

Beverages   11%

Dairy Products   11%

Other Foods   5%

nals of pleasure our brains will discharge as a reward for choosing something yummy. Nutrition is rarely the most important factor on our minds when we choose our food. More often it's the taste, the flavor, the expected sensory satisfaction, the emotion tied up with eating the same snack that your mom served you when you got home from school when you were six. All these conscious, subconscious, and nearly spiritual thoughts and feelings flood the brain in a matter of milliseconds, and you make a decision.[1]

How Big Food Targets and Influences the Consumer

As powerful as riskily altered ingredients can be when fully titrated and tested for optimal mouthfeel and emotional release, the ingredients are just part of the Big Food battle plan. Marketing is equally as important.

In recent years, the biggest American food companies have been sued for using food marketing terms like *natural* and *all-natural*. More than two hundred class-action suits have been filed against Big Food companies, alleging that they misused the adjective in marketing such appetizing oxymora as "natural" Cheetos Puffs, "all-natural" Sun Chips, "all-natural" Naked Juice, and "100 percent all-natural" Tyson chicken nuggets, to name just a few. Many of these products contain artificial flavors, preservatives, synthetic ingredients, and high-fructose corn syrup—not stuff that typically fits the "natural" bill.[2]

The pushing of boundaries becomes even more shocking once you realize that kids are one of the main targets of Big Food marketing efforts. Let's take Kraft's TV dinner–like tray of meat and cheese, Lunchables, an iconic giant among convenience foods that radically changed the eating habits of millions of American kids, as a case in point.

My oldest daughter is now almost three years old. She goes to day care, and one of my daily chores at home is getting her lunch ready for the next day. I have gotten my routine down to where it only takes me five minutes to get her lunch ready—grapes, mozzarella cheese stick, yogurt, and some combination of rice or pasta with chicken or fish or veggies. Five minutes might not seem like that much time, but if you multiply five minutes per day by five days per week, that's almost twenty-two hours per year I spend prepping my kid's lunch! Would I love a convenient, affordable, and nutritious alternative so that I could spend those twenty-two hours reading, working, watching Netflix, or just zoning out? Yes, please!

Lunchables are a marketing dynamo designed to make the lives of working parents easier while playing off kids' burgeoning need for freedom and fun. The ready-to-eat meals include meat, cheese, crackers, and candy, allowing kids to assemble them in whatever combination they desire. Food marketers use psychological targeting to deliver the advertising that surrounds Lunchables.

If you pay a visit to the Lunchables website, first what you'll notice is that they split their audience into "Kids" and "Parents"—you have to choose one path before advancing to the home page. At the top left of the Kids page is a banner in small font that sneakily proclaims, "This Is Advertising." And in even tinier font at the bottom of the Kids section is a little disclaimer that says, "The games and other activities on this website include messages about the products Kraft sells." The entire kids' portal is not overtly about food, but rather an app-based game called "K-Catch: An Inter-Dimensional Puzzle Revolution." The game is filled with flying processed food characters who make Lunchables seem like a lovable character you might find in a bedtime story.

The parents' side of the house doesn't have any video games, but it does have a lot of fantasy-inspired pseudonyms for riskily altered food. Lunchables has expanded their repertoire since I was a kid and now offers several dozen varietals on the original Light Bologna & American Cracker Stackers. In reaction to parental outrage over sugar water and cookies for lunch five days per week, recently Lunchables launched their health-washed "Lunchables with 100% JUICE" line. Their Chicken Popper Kabobbles meal is representative of how riskily altered provisions are often marketed as real, nutritious food.

First off, what the hell is a Kabobble? This reminds me of my rib-shaped pork patty MRE days—and that is not a good thing.

Second, Kraft proclaims that the Lunchable is "an excellent source of protein," and there is a big sticker on the meal box that says, "Made with REAL FRUIT." You have to read the fine print to see that the JUICE touted in capital letters is actually "Fruit punch flavored 100% juice blend from concentrate with added ingredient and other natural flavor." No mention of what "added ingredient" or "natural flavor" is or why the grammar is worse than that of the Indonesian eighth graders I taught in Java. If you only had ten seconds to buy the product while shopping with two screaming kids in your shopping cart, fat chance you would have the patience or the time to understand what kind of riskily altered food you were about to feed your children.

"Your Typical Consumers Don't Stand a Chance"

I wanted to understand how Big Food marketers think about marketing to kids, so I spoke with Bruce Bradley. Bruce spent over fifteen years working as a marketing executive at some of the biggest processed-food brands in the world, including Nabisco, Pillsbury, and General Mills. "Only by taking a hard look at the industry and detaching myself from the culture of Big Food did I finally conclude that your typical consumers don't stand a chance against the marketing muscle of food companies," says Bruce. "And that realization is what got me actively blogging, agreeing to interviews, and pulling back the curtain on Big Food's long track record of deception."[3]

I asked Bruce about the most shocking food marketing tactic he ever saw employed, and he immediately started talking about Frosted Flakes. "What gets me the most angry is when I see junk food marketed to kids as a healthy choice. Probably the example that gets under my skin the most is Kellogg's Frosted Flakes. With the help of Tony the Tiger, Frosted Flakes has been marketed to generations of kids as a good choice for kids to start their day. Honestly, there's very little nutritionally redeeming about Frosted Flakes, yet Kellogg's tells kids that Frosted Flakes 'fuels them up to be their best.' Unfortunately, nothing could be further from the truth! And by peddling highly processed, sugary products to kids, food manufacturers are teaching our youth the most unhealthy food habits possible that have the potential to lead to lifelong struggles with weight and a whole host of chronic diseases."[4]

When Bruce elaborates, you can tell he is still paying penance for a career spent convincing kids to consume. Bruce tells me that with the help of advertising agencies, research firms, and brand character specialists, Big Food companies launch advertising smart bombs, disguised as fun-loving characters, straight at kids. Is it a fair fight? "I don't think so," says Bruce. "Winning the hearts, minds, and stomachs of consumers is no small feat, so Big Food manufacturers have to pull out all the stops. Unfortunately, kids get caught in the crossfire."[5]

Kids spend more than $200 billion annually, and they influence many food purchases beyond those they make directly. Although kids' choices are strongly influenced by their parents and siblings, they are increasingly making decisions at younger ages, either in ways that are independent of parental guidance or as agents influencing the choices and purchasing decisions of their parents and caregivers—"More SpongeBob Cheez-Its, please, Mom!"

Of the various items that kids purchase and influence, food and beverages—particularly candy, carbonated soft drinks, and salty snacks—consistently represent the leading categories. The food industry spends a massive amount of money—almost $2 billion—to get kids to eat and drink more sugary drinks, sugary cereals, sweet and salty snacks, and fast food. Advertisers spend roughly $950 million annually on television tailored to children under twelve, according to industry estimates.[6] Less than $10 million is spent marketing healthy foods like fruits and vegetables to kids.[7]

Food marketing to children has been identified as playing a key role in the national obesity crisis facing American children today. The National Academies' Institute of Medicine, for example, has compiled studies that show the importance of television advertisements in influencing unhealthy food and beverage preferences, requests, and diets of children. A recent comprehensive review by the Institute of Medicine demonstrated that despite efforts to decrease obesity and increase healthy eating, television food advertising was still negatively affecting children's food choices, diets, and health.[8]

Public health professionals are not only concerned about the quantity and types of advertising targeted at children and youth, they are also alarmed about the nutritional quality of products most heavily marketed to children. Despite some improvements in recent years, the overwhelming majority of food and beverage advertising targeted to the young still tends to be for products of poor nutritional quality. For example, the Federal Trade Commission (FTC) reported that in 2009, food and beverage companies spent $1.79 billion to market their products to kids. Seventy-two percent of this total was spent to market just three types of products: breakfast cereals, fast foods, and carbonated drinks.[9]

Teenagers are even juicier targets than the Frosted Flakes– and Lunchables-age crowd. Starting in middle school, kids have more money and freedom. This is also when kids begin to form the preferences and dislikes that will define them for the rest of their lives. Food marketers also specifically target low-income neighborhoods and black and Latino kids. This means that some kids get a "double dose" of marketing—in the media and in their own neighborhoods. As a kid, where your parents live and how much money they make has a direct impact on what marketing you are exposed to.[10]

Big Food continues to aggressively market its least nutritious products directly to children. As a recent report on cereal marketing concludes, "Companies do offer more nutritious and lower-sugar cereals for children, like regular Cheerios and Frosted Mini-Wheats, but they are marketed to parents, not children."[11]

"While cereal companies have made small improvements to the nutrition of their child-targeted cereals, these cereals are still far worse than the products they market to adults. They have 56 percent more sugar, half as much fiber, and 5 percent more sodium," said cereal marketing report coauthor Marlene Schwartz, deputy director of the Rudd Center for Food Policy and Obesity. "The companies know how to make a range of good-tasting cereals that aren't loaded with sugar and salt. Why can't they help parents out and market these directly to children instead?"

"It is obvious that industry regulating itself is a failure. If there is to be any hope of protecting children from predatory marketing, either public outcry or government action will be necessary to force

the companies to change," added coauthor Kelly Brownell, director of the Rudd Center.[12]

How Big Food Manufactures Health Claims

Big Food marketing power becomes clear when you look at the hundreds of millions of dollars that are spent advertising products
every year. A few examples:

1. *McDonald's spent $115 million just to market Happy Meals.*[13]

2. *General Mills spent $73.7 million advertising Honey Nut Cheerios,
   $29 million for Cinnamon Toast Crunch, and $12.6 million on
   Lucky Charms.*[14]

3. *Frito-Lay spent almost $150 million advertising Cheetos, Doritos,
   and other chips.*[15]

These are astronomical sums. But if you are a Big Food marketing
executive, there's one big problem—the ads are blatantly obvious,
and they are becoming less effective as potential target customers
migrate from TV to mobile and from magazines to social media. Traditional food marketing still gets the message across and drives
sales, but there is increasing resistance and skepticism toward advertising, particularly when it involves marketing to children.

Michael Mudd is a former executive vice president of global corporate affairs for Kraft Foods. He retired in 2004. In a 2013 opinion piece for *The New York Times*, Michael wrote, "I was part of the
packaged food and beverage business for more than twenty years.
As the national waistline grew, the industry sought refuge in the fact
that the obesity epidemic has many causes. It has insistently used
that fact to fight off government regulators and justify why it should
not have to change what it sells or how it sells it."[16]

Big Food often blurs the line between science and marketing.

"Objective science" is conducted and then expertly spun into marketing, almost always cloaked by Big Food institutes (e.g., Coca-Cola's Beverage Institute for Health and Wellness, General Mills' Bell Institute, and Nestlé's Nutrition Institute). A doctor's stamp of approval works magic when you have only a fraction of a second to make a buying decision.

As a recent *New York Times* article on the war between the sugar and high-fructose corn syrup trade groups stated, "academic experts frequently become extensions of corporate lobbying campaigns as rival industries use them to try to inflict damage on their competitors or defend their reputations."[17]

With one foot in the world of science and one foot in the world of marketing spin, how is a time-crunched consumer supposed to know which way is up?

How the Nutritional Guidelines Have Led Us Astray

In the early 1980s, Luise Light was teaching at New York University when she was recruited to work for the U.S. Department of Agriculture (USDA). As the director of dietary guidance and nutrition education research, Light was asked to create a new set of guidelines for food in order to help consumers navigate the confusing world of health and nutrition claims.[18]

Light and her team developed the concept of the Food Pyramid. Her version of the pyramid promoted a diet based on fruits and vegetables. Lean meats and fish came next. And grains and sugars were placed near the top, where only limited amounts were recommended. Having devoted her life to the study of nutrition, Light knew that the human body is not designed to live primarily on the nutrients from breads and processed carbohydrates. That is how the Food Pyramid was originally submitted to the authorities within the USDA. The USDA loved the idea of the Food Pyramid. And they were thrilled with the simplicity of the design.[19]

But when Light saw her pyramid in its final form, she was appalled. As Light recounts, "When our version of the Food Guide came back to us revised, we were shocked to find that it was vastly different from the one we had developed."[20]

The first USDA food guide, "Food for Young Children," appeared in 1916. Foods were categorized into five groups: milk and meat, cereals, vegetables and fruits, fats and fatty foods, and sugars and sugary foods. This food guide was followed in 1917 by dietary recommendations also based on these five food groups, targeted to the general public in "How to Select Foods."[21]

The USDA guides evolved slowly over the next seven decades, until 1992, when based on Light's concept, the USDA created a powerful icon: the Food Guide Pyramid. This simple illustration conveyed what the USDA said were the elements of a healthy diet. However, as the Matzner Clinic points out, the information embodied in this pyramid was based on shaky scientific evidence, and it was seldom updated to reflect major advances in our understanding of the connection between diet and health.[22]

A healthy diet, by definition, had suddenly become a low-fat diet. Eating too many calories was the problem, and since fat contains more than twice as many calories per gram as either protein or carbohydrates, "people who cut down on fat usually lose weight," as *The Washington Post* reported in 1985. As Gary Taubes reported in *Good Calories, Bad Calories*, beginning in the late 1980s with the publication of the Food Guide Pyramid and *The Surgeon General's Report on Nutrition and Health*, an entire research industry arose to create acceptable nonfat fat substitutes, while the food industry spent billions of dollars marketing the "less-fat-is-good-health" message. The USDA's pyramid and booklet on dietary guidelines recommended that fats and oils be eaten "sparingly," while we were now to eat six to eleven servings per day of the pasta, potatoes, rice, and bread once considered uniquely fattening.[23]

The focus shifted from obtaining adequate nutrients through a well-rounded mix of real food, to avoiding excessive intakes of certain food groups (particularly fats) that were spuriously linked to chronic diseases.[24] Fat became evil, almost literally overnight. Americans were encouraged to use vegetable oils instead of butter, which prompted food manufacturers to create hardened oils through the hydrogenated process so they resembled butter. Margarine rapidly gained ground in our diets; at the turn of the century, people consumed only two pounds per person per year, but by the 1990s, people were eating around eight pounds.[25]

Scientists tried to correlate a fatty diet to fatty arteries, as deaths from coronary artery disease (CAD) began to climb. According to what would come to be known as the diet-heart hypothesis, saturated fat raises blood cholesterol levels and leads to the buildup of cholesterol and other fats as plaques in the arteries. To bolster this theory, a University of Minnesota public health researcher named Ancel Keys showed a nearly direct correlation between calories from fat in the diet and deaths from heart disease among populations across seven countries.[26]

According to Dr. David Perlmutter, the only problem with Keys's analysis is that he ignored countries that didn't fit this pattern, including many where people eat a lot of fat but don't get heart disease and others where the diets are low in fat yet their populations have a high incidence of fatal heart attacks. The Japanese, whose diets have only 10 percent of calories coming from fat, showed the lowest CAD mortality—less than one in one thousand. The United States, on the other hand, had the highest CAD mortality (seven in one thousand) with 40 percent of its calories coming from fat. On the surface, it would seem that these patterns point directly to the idea that fat is bad and that fat causes heart disease. Keys made international headlines and even appeared on the cover of *Time* magazine. Health officials, scientists, and the American public bought the "fat is bad" story hook, line, and sinker. Little did we know then that the data wasn't telling the whole story.[27]

Health authorities began to advise people to replace these "bad fats" with carbohydrates and processed polyunsaturated vegetable oils, including soybean and corn oils. Fast-food restaurants followed suit in the mid-1980s, switching from beef fat and palm oil to partially hydrogenated (trans fat) vegetable oil to fry their foods. Even though the USDA has since converted its food guide from a pyramid to a plate, it still communicates the idea that "fat is bad" and "carbs are good." In fact, the new MyPlate doesn't feature fats at all, "making it very confusing for consumers to know how fats fit into a healthy diet, if at all."[28] Walter Willett, chairman of the Harvard School for Public Health's nutrition department, says, "The pyramid really ignored forty years of data and condemned all fats and oils."[29]

Luise Light recounts,

As I later discovered, the wholesale changes made to [our] guide by the Office of the Secretary of Agriculture were calculated to win the acceptance of the food industry. For instance, the Ag Secretary's office altered wording to emphasize processed foods over fresh and whole foods, to downplay lean meats and low-fat dairy choices because the meat and milk lobbies believed it'd hurt sales of full-fat products; it also hugely increased the servings of wheat and other grains to make the wheat growers happy. The meat lobby got the final word on the color of the saturated fat / cholesterol guideline, which was changed from red to purple because meat producers worried that using red to signify "bad" fat would be linked to red meat in consumers' minds.[30]

Light continues,

Where we, the USDA nutritionists, called for a base of 5–9 servings of fresh fruits and vegetables a day, it was replaced with a paltry 2–3 servings. Our recommendation of 3–4 daily servings of whole-grain breads and cereals was changed to a whopping 6–11 servings forming the base of the Food Pyramid as a concession to the processed wheat and corn industries.

Moreover, my nutritionist group had placed baked goods made with white flour—including crackers, sweets and other low-nutrient foods laden with sugars and fats—at the peak of the pyramid, recommending that they be eaten sparingly. To our alarm, in the "revised" Food Guide, they were now made part of the Pyramid's base. And, in yet one more assault on dietary logic, changes were made to the wording of the dietary guidelines from "eat less" to "avoid too much," giving a nod to the processed-food industry interests by not limiting highly profitable "fun foods" (junk foods by any other name) that might affect the bottom line of food companies.[31]

When Things Get Complicated, We Fail

Surprisingly, the more time I spent researching and thinking about how to eat better, the more confused I became. I learned that nutrition science is still very primitive—and is a very complex and difficult discipline.

I wanted to understand on a fundamental level what and how I should be eating, but the complexity created through marketing spin, faulty science, and bad data left me overweight, confused, and stressed. Many industry insiders have intentionally overcomplicated things—and when things get complicated, we often fail.

At Plated, our Third Core Belief is: *People succeed when it's easier to do the right thing than the wrong thing.* The preponderance of food marketing and complicated nutrition messages over the last forty years has left many of us baffled. We don't even know how to determine right from wrong!

At Plated, we are trying to be deliberate and conscious as we evolve our business to make it easier to make good food decisions. Health will always be an intensely personal endeavor, but we think we can build a better, more transparent, more successful food model by sticking to our core beliefs.

Chapter 7

When Food Becomes Nutrition

One-liner: The future of food, nutrition, and health is coming. However, because nutrition science is still relatively primitive and complex, it's easy to drive yourself crazy, so be careful.

Let me start off by saying that there are an infinite number of ways to drive yourself nuts, but doing what I did is a surefire path to obsessive compulsion, neuroses, and locking yourself in a room in a quest for "truth." I wish I were charitable enough to say that I suffered through what you're about to read so that you don't have to, but in reality, my quest to get to the heart of nutrition was much more selfish than that. I just wanted to look good, feel good, and have six-pack abs. Where I wound up was locked in a hyperbaric chamber for twenty-four hours having my metabolism monitored by a team of Columbia Ph.D.s.

But there is a silver lining here, and it's this:

I learned that at this point in human history, we do not yet have the capabilities to quantify the self to the extent needed to tailor optimal nutrition, health, and living for each and every person. We will get there soon (within the next decade or two), and in this chapter, we'll meet some of the pioneers who are creating the road map for the quantified self. But in the interim, because we don't have the answers, let's not pretend like we do.

We all need to do our own research and testing to figure out what blend of nutrition, stress, sleep, and exercise works best for each one of us as individuals—there is no one-size-fits-all approach, and there are no shortcuts. But at a certain point, I found that it's "healthier" to pull back from the brink of obsession and to return to treating food as food and not nutrition—life is just too short.

But before we get ahead of ourselves, let's start at the beginning.

From the Marines to Man Breasts

When I started working on this book in the fall of 2015, my wife and I were expecting our second daughter, my cofounder Josh and I had been in crunch mode on the business for four years, and I was 228 pounds with 27 percent body fat. I was 30 pounds heavier than I'd been just a few years earlier in the Marines, and I realized that I felt gross for the first time in a long time. I was running a food business with the mission of making good food a reality for everyone, but I had been so focused on business and family that I had lost perspective on my own well-being.

Since high school, I had always prided myself on being an athlete, and while I was in the Marines, I consistently scored perfect 300s on the physical fitness test—20 pull-ups, 100 sit-ups in under two minutes, and three miles of running in under eighteen minutes.

But here I was, 1.5 kids, a wife, and a business later, and I was well on the way to a flabby, pasty, man-breasted #DadBod.

If you have kids or know anyone who does, you know that the first few years (I hope it's only the first few years!) are pretty insane. All my good habits (sleeping, exercising, eating real adult food, not living on a steady drip of caffeine) went out the window. I was also working sixty-, seventy-, and sometimes eighty-plus-hour weeks. I was running a business whose mission and ethos was based around healthy and sustainable eating, but I had put myself on a course for obesity and early-onset diabetes.

What the hell happened to me?

Navigating the World of Nutrition "Science"

I wanted to learn more about the science of nutrition, so I turned to the smartest expert in the field: Google. I searched "How do I learn more about nutrition?" and I hovered on the first link that I was served—the Institute for Integrative Nutrition. I clicked through and immediately became skeptical.

The institute bills itself as "the world's largest nutrition school and certification program, empowering people to transform the world." I signed up for the institute's newsletter, and received a "personal" e-mail from the founder. He explained that the institute's mission was "to play a crucial role in improving health and happiness, and through that process, create a ripple effect that transforms the world." He encouraged me, "I want you to know that you have the strength, power, and passion to become the healthiest and happiest you've ever been in your life. You can overcome whatever is holding you back. Whatever it may be, you have the power to make a difference." I felt like I had fallen into the clutches of what happens when Groupon and Deepak Chopra make a baby. The institute proclaims that it was also named one of the healthiest companies in America, so if they got that right, they must be legit![1]

Optimizing happiness and longevity is complex, and there are a lot of charlatans out there who conflate nutrition and getting the most out of life. My introduction to the institute is just one real, if slightly new age and hilarious, example of the conversation that surrounds nutrition science. Many of these practitioners believe fully what they're preaching, but their wholehearted belief systems mostly ignore or only pay lip service to the real science that drives most other twenty-first-century disciplines.[2]

The problem is that as humans, we all eat every day. I mean, that's not a problem more broadly—if it were truly a problem, we wouldn't have a business. It's a problem because we are all intimately familiar with food, and as a consequence, it is really easy to make nutritional guidance anecdotal. After all, eating is pretty important, and we tend to care a lot about what we eat. So if you're on a strict low-carb diet, you are more likely to recommend a low-carb approach to anyone uninitiated enough to ask for your advice.

Additionally, like any discipline or industry, there are also professional pressures and expectations. Someone who studies a particular food likely has preconceptions about what he or she expects the food to do to health. A professor attempting to get tenure is under pressure to come up with fundable and noteworthy results. Researchers who built their careers on demonizing or applauding particular foods have a vested interest in substantiating their views.[3]

In the Marine Corps, our infantry instructors constantly talked about "human factors"—hunger, stress, sleep deprivation, extreme heat or cold—as determining more battles than bullets or bombs. It turns out when you're tired, cold, stressed, and hungry, you don't fight as well. Fancy that.

A different set of human factors, but human factors nonetheless, can influence how science is done. There is even a term for this— white hat bias: "Bias leading to distortion of information in the service of what may be perceived to be righteous ends." For example, for someone who has committed her career to fighting obesity, a statistically significant change in weight, no matter how small, may be used to further a policy agenda.[4]

Building legitimate evidence, discussing the evidence, and using the evidence are three very different disciplines. The first two are where science can and should play the role of pushing our collective human knowledge forward. But unfortunately, when it comes to nutrition, more often than not, steps one and two get skipped, and evidence gets trundled out as dogma. Time and again, since everybody eats and since we are all looking for nutrition guidance, half-baked science gets repurposed as BuzzFeed clickbait, and next thing you know, everyone and your long-lost half sister Mildred are choking down turmeric juice cleanses.

It doesn't need to be this way.

Do We Know What Makes Us Healthy?

Why is it that what we are advised with confidence to eat one year is so often reversed the next? We go from "Red meat is the root of all evils!" to "Eat like a caveman!" And from "Egg yolks will kill you!" to "Eat more egg yolks!" The simplest explanation for the bipolar nature of nutrition guidance is that—drumroll, please—it is just how science works.

An observation leads to a hypothesis. The hypothesis ("Egg yolks will kill you!") gets tested, and it fails the new test. Keep in mind: Failure is always the most likely outcome in any scientific experiment. There are an infinite number of wrong hypotheses for every right one—so the odds are always against any particular hypothesis being true, no matter how obvious it might seem. Hypotheses begin their transformation into policy recommendations only after they've received support from a field of research known as epidemiology. Epidemiology is the study of epidemics—you probably don't need a degree in Greek and Latin roots to solve that one. For seven decades, epidemiology has been used to find the causes of cancer, heart disease, and the other main chronic diseases that end up killing most of us.[5]

But here's the rub: We have almost certainly overestimated what epidemiologic research can actually accomplish. The case of red meat and saturated fat causing heart disease is just one of many examples where epidemiology has fallen short. But it proves an important point: Trying to establish reliable scientific knowledge is incredibly hard when the research tools themselves are broken.[6]

The cohort study deserves much of the blame for the bad epidemiological science we have witnessed since the 1950s. In these studies, the scientists monitor disease rates and lifestyle factors (diet, physical activity, prescription drug use, exposure to stress, etc.) in or between large populations (oftentimes featuring tens or hundreds of thousands of people). These studies can cost millions of dollars and can take decades to perform fully.

Scientists then try to develop hypotheses about what caused the results. Since so much time and money is often invested, and since the diseases under observation are epidemic by definition, results generate fiendish coverage from the media. From the benefits of avocados to the dangers of caffeine and sitting at work, these cohort studies provide the only available data outside the laboratory on critical issues impacting hundreds of millions of people's lives.

The dangerous game being played here, as David Sackett, a retired Oxford University epidemiologist, has observed, is the presumption of preventive medicine. "The goal of the endeavor is to tell those of us who are otherwise in fine health how to remain healthy longer." But this assumes that the hypotheses and recommendations prevent rather than cause problems. Remember how we were told to eat margarine in the 1980s? Now it turns out that margarine actually causes cancer. Whoops!

Nothing illustrates this better than a classic 2012 systematic review in *The American Journal of Clinical Nutrition* that pretty much showed that everything we eat is associated with both higher and lower rates of cancer.[7] With the presumption of "do no harm," how clear does the data have to be before any advice is offered?

The issue with cohort studies is that no matter how well designed and how many hundreds of thousands of subjects they might include, they still have a fundamental constraint—what they call at Harvard Business School the ol' correlation-causation conundrum. They actually don't call it that—I just made that up. But it definitely is a conundrum.

Cohort studies can distinguish correlations between two events—that men who eat less saturated fat *have* less heart disease, for example. But they cannot determine causation—the conclusion that one event *causes* the other; that eating less saturated fat *protects against* heart disease. As a result, observational studies can only provide what researchers call "hypothesis-generating evidence"—what our general counsel would call "circumstantial evidence." Testing these hypotheses in any definitive way requires a randomized-controlled trial (RCT)—an experiment, not an observational study. Not only are RCTs even more expensive and time consuming than cohort studies, but they also have the nasty habit of providing the "back" to the back-and-forth of epidemiological recommendations.[8]

Understanding the limitations of epidemiology is the easy part. The RCTs needed to develop bulletproof data about a lifestyle or diet change are insanely expensive and time consuming—a recent review of RCTs conducted by the National Institutes of Health put the average cost at $12 million. By randomly assigning people into a diet intervention group or a placebo group, these trials "control" for all other possible variables that might affect the outcome, like the weight or household income of the participants. This is why randomized trials, particularly those known as placebo-controlled, double-blind trials, are typically considered the gold standard for establishing reliable data about whether a diet is actually safe and effective.[9]

But RCTs also have limitations beyond the investment of time and money. They can't be used to study suspected harmful effects. Imagine the uproar that would be caused by subjecting thousands of people to a diet heavy in an ingredient that is known to cause cancer. First, it would never pass an ethics review board. Second, no one would ever fund such a thing. And third, even if you *could* pull off one and two, you'd probably get murdered by the offspring of thousands of people to whom you knowingly gave cancer. Not a pretty picture.

And even when RCTs do get funded and approved, it's hard to determine how the results apply on an individual level. RCTs tend to attract people who are motivated to volunteer and will follow the prescribed protocol for years. Consequently, RCTs "are very good for showing that a drug does what the pharmaceutical company says it does," David Atkins, a preventive-medicine specialist at the Agency for Healthcare Research and Quality, says, "but not very good for telling you how big the benefit really is and what are the harms in typical people. Because they don't enroll typical people."[10]

So is there no way to study nutrition with real, hard-core, convincing science? I reconnected with one of my best buddies from college, Lance Martin, the one who had just received his Ph.D. in applied physics and bioengineering at Stanford, whom we met earlier on.

Lance explained that historically there has always been an interest in studying microbial metabolism—how different bugs metabolize things. Bugs are very trackable systems—you can grow them in a dish, knock out their genes, mess with them, and study them closely. Therefore, there's been interest in how metabolism works in different microorganisms and simple organisms like bugs.

But the human metabolic system is much more complex than what you study in a lab—and that makes a big difference. Researchers like to work with "model systems," science jargon for a particular species that has been developed over many years to be conducive to experiments, a system that can be tinkered with to test specific theories and answer specific questions—think lab rats and fruit flies. Humans are not a model system. You can culture human cells, but nutrition is a complex thing. Studies would require re-creating the human stomach in isolation, which sounds scary and vaguely reminiscent of Krang from *Teenage Mutant Ninja Turtles*.

It's a hard problem to work on from a reductionist, scientific standpoint. How would you design a really high-end research program around human nutrition? What would be the model systems you work with? How would you run experiments? Every person is so different, and the human gut is very complicated.

Lance also pointed to another potentially even larger issue: Where's the funding and excitement for this kind of scientific research? The funding is not going to nutrition and wellness—it's going to cancer and heart disease. As Lance told me, "The biology of cancer is incredibly appealing to researchers. It's a disease driven by genetics with a clear mechanism of action and clear mutations." The big, sexy venture capital funding goes to research on very acute human diseases, like cancer and heart disease, even though at this point it has been proven that poor nutrition leads to increased incidences of both. As a result, most of the bioengineers, big data folks, and the other hotshot scientists go to work on problems like biotech and cancer and very few of the world's geniuses are focusing on nutrition.

Nina Teicholz, the investigative journalist who authored a bestselling tome called *The Big Fat Surprise*, agrees. In the book, she writes about the "enduring problem of nutrition science: much of it turns out to be highly fallible." At the heart of every scientific study is one goal: to measure what people eat and then follow them over a period of years to monitor their health. And, like Lance pointed out, there are a billion other factors that could be affecting their health.

"While good science should be ruled by skepticism and self-doubt," Teicholz says, "the field of nutrition has instead been shaped by passions verging on zealotry."[11]

So if epidemiology is broken, and RCTs are expensive, time consuming, and inherently flawed, and the human body isn't a model system, and nutrition science is a murky field where data is hard to come by, and the data that *does* exist is often used in conflicting ways by different authors and pundits trying to make a point, then where should we turn for advice and guidance on how we should be eating? As I discovered, and I don't mean this in a new age way, the answer lies within us already.

The Future of Nutrition

Within the medical community, the move to electronic medical records and the use of digital biomedical measurement devices is already transforming how doctors think and work. In addition to this formal evolution, there is an early, amateur-led grassroots movement to "quantify" nutrition and its impact. I decided to take a plunge into the world of the "quantified self" in an effort to get to the root of what and how I should be eating for an optimal life.

I talked with dozens of biologists, cancer researchers, computer scientists, physiologists, and amateur biohackers, and I cobbled together their insight and advice to start tracking many of my own biomarkers. Through my blood, urine, saliva, and stool, I was able to gain insight into the status of major subsystems of my body. I then layered in tools to help interpret these results through the lenses of my own genome and the microbes in my gut. And in the process, I lost over thirty pounds, I dropped my body fat percentage to single digits, and I reached a level of energy and fitness that I hadn't felt since college.

Even though I am a far cry from a medical professional, I was able to use commercially available tests and a "systems biology integrative approach" to quantifying my nutrition and myself. I have become an early example of the American biology legend Leroy Hood's vision of the "predictive, preventive, personalized, and participatory approach" to health care, what he called P4 medicine. This is where the future of nutrition and medicine *will* be; it's not an *if*, but a *when*. However, we are not there yet, and my story should also serve as a cautionary tale of what can happen when we allow food to become nothing more than nutrition. Let's jump in!

Bionic Man: Dr. Larry Smarr

I started my quantified-self journey talking about the bowel movements of a sixty-eight-year-old celebrity scientist. "Do you realize how data-rich your poop is?" Dr. Larry Smarr and I had been talking on the phone for all of five minutes, and we were already deep into his literal shit. "There are about 100 billion bacteria per gram. Each bacterium has DNA whose length is typically one to 10 megabases—call it 1 million bytes of information. This means human stool has a data capacity of 100,000 terabytes of information stored per gram. That's many orders of magnitude more information density than, say, in a chip in your smartphone or your personal computer. So your stool is far more interesting than a computer."[12]

And Larry knows a thing or two about computers. He led a team of scientists who connected supercomputers across the United States in the early 1980s to create one of the earliest versions of what today we call the Internet. Today, he leads a futuristic research center at the University of California–San Diego, called the California Institute for Telecommunications and Information Technology, or Calit2. Over the last fifteen years, Larry has attracted almost a billion dollars in private, public, and nonprofit funding to fuel his research.

At Calit2, Larry and his team "basically live in the future." Larry says his eyes are focused "ten years ahead," which in computer terms is more like a century, given how rapidly technology is transforming our world. "For instance," he told me, "last year Facebook bought Oculus Rift for $2 billion, so now everybody is talking about virtual reality. Well, we've been building virtual reality facilities for over thirty years—with much higher resolution. I'm talking about walk-in rooms that are virtual reality.

"As the takeoff to the broad-based consumer market happens, we have had thirty years of experience with how humans interact in virtual reality, how to generate content for virtual reality, how to do collaborative projects jointly across the country and the world within a shared virtual reality. So we have been living in the future of the broad consumer market for decades. That is what we like to do. And right now, we are working on the human gut and analyzing how particularly the microbiome changes with disease and with respect to food."[13]

Larry envisions a coming revolution in how we use our own bodies to practice preventative medicine, primarily through a more scientific, personalized, and quantified approach to nutrition. He is conducting a computer-aided study of his own body and has gone so far as to publish a "how-to guide" for quantifying your body "from a systems biology perspective."[14]

In Larry's vision, we will all have "a working model of your unique corpus, grounded in your own genome, and—using data collected by nanosensors and transmitted by smartphone—refreshed continually with measurements from your body's insides. This information stream will be collated with similar readings from millions of other similarly monitored bodies all over the planet. Mining this enormous database, software will produce detailed guidance about diet, supplements, exercise, medication, or treatment—guidance based not on the current practice of lumping symptoms together into broad categories of disorders but on a precise reading of your own body's peculiarities and its status in real time."[15]

Larry is using his own body (what he calls his "ecosystem") and the data it generates to prove what is possible at the frontier of nutrition, technology, and medicine. And this is not just academic, self-experimental fun: Larry used this approach—his own data plus a doctor's advice—to diagnose a life-threatening disease before he even started feeling any symptoms.

In 2010, Larry had already radically changed his diet. Following Barry Sears's Zone Diet, he had dropped twenty pounds. While Larry was happy with this weight loss, his dieting taught him something: If you want good health, you can't just blindly trust how you feel.

Larry knew that he had to examine the data to get to a root cause understanding of what was happening in his body. Calit2 already had numerous grants to study "digitally enabled genomic medicine," so in 2010, Larry signed himself up as a test subject. As he told me, "I turned my body into a genetic observatory, taking sequential blood and stool samples as often as every day. Now I've got over 4.5 years of data in detail. I've got 150 blood variables that I track every month to quarter. So for the first time, you are able to actually see how a human body tracks dynamically in terms of the underlying system variables." As his personal quest to lose weight evolved into an effort to understand human biochemistry, his own body became the equivalent of a data-enabled petri dish.

And something wasn't adding up. Despite his weight loss, the data was now telling him that the pounds should still have been falling off, but they weren't. The Zone Diet is designed to reduce inflammation, and because he strictly followed it, Larry expected his inflammation score to be low. But the C-reactive protein (CRP) score, which rises in response to inflammation, was high.

"I had discovered that my body is chronically inflamed—just the opposite of what I expected!" he wrote in an account of his project published in 2011 in a special issue of *Strategic News Service*, an industry newsletter. Larry wrote, "Even more intriguing: after I had been tracking my CRP for two years, I noticed that it had suddenly more than doubled in less than a year. Troubled, I showed my graphs to my doctors and suggested that something bad was about to happen."

Imagine walking into your doctor's office with a rucksack filled with printed charts, stool samples, blood vials, and a suspicion that you're sick. The only catch is that you don't feel sick. So your doctor tells you to go home, get some sleep, and stop worrying. Someone once asked Larry if he is a hypochondriac. "A hypochondriac is someone who imagines that they have things that are wrong with them and worries about that," he says. "I am the opposite of a hypochondriac. I don't make any assumptions about what might be right or wrong with me, and I don't imagine it. I measure it." The doctors sent Larry home and told him to come back if he actually had a problem, not a hypothesis driven from data analysis.

This is the fundamental problem with how medicine works today: It treats symptoms. Medicine doesn't prevent illness using rigorous data analysis. Larry was beginning to have serious doubts about his doctors. "Here's the way I look at it: The average American has something like two twenty-minute visits a year with a doctor," he explains. "So you have forty minutes a year that that doctor is going to help you make good decisions. You have five hundred thousand minutes a year on your own, and every one of those, you are making decisions. So we're already in a situation where you are in charge of your ship—your body—and you are making a lot of pretty horrible decisions, or else two-thirds of the United States' citizens wouldn't be overweight or obese. You wouldn't have the CDC saying that 42 percent of Americans may be obese by 2030, and a third of all Americans may develop diabetes by 2050. That's the result of a lot of bad decisions that people are individually making on their own."

A month or so after his doctor sent him home, Larry felt severe pain in his belly. He returned to the doctor and was now diagnosed with an intestinal infection and prescribed antibiotics. Larry had predicted a problem using his own data, but modern medicine had fallen short. Fed up, Larry decided to take matters into his own hands.

He requested a new colonoscopy and began testing his stool. This work led him to realize that humans are actually complex ecosystems, or superorganisms. He told me, "We are talking about insane biodiversity here. All animals that you know of—from goldfish to elephants to humans—are vertebrates, and that is a subbiome of life on earth. Insects are a whole different biome, plants are a different biome, and so forth. There are six to eight biomes of life inside of your large intestine! So your gut is more diverse than a coral reef plus a rainforest plus an insectarium. Each one of us is a walking ecology of vast biodiversity, and we've only just started to understand what this means."

Larry's stool samples provided information on the microorganisms inhabiting his gut, which is what Larry means when he calls his poop "data-rich." The numbers continued to tell a bad story. They suggested that he was suffering not from an infection but from some kind of inflamed-bowel disease.

Larry's quest for the quantified self ultimately led him to an early diagnosis of Crohn's disease. Crohn's is not fatal, but it is incurable, and it comes with a bunch of symptoms that can be uncomfortable and painful. Apart from that one episode of abdominal pain, Larry was still feeling fine. But the graphs showed, and his new doctor more or less confirmed, that he was sick.

In the near future (Larry would say the future is already here), data will help people recognize disease long before they feel sick. Doctors will move from being the CEO of your health to serving more as operational consultants or how we think of financial advisors today. Instead of being responsible for the management of your health, primarily by reacting to crises, doctors instead will analyze the data and will help plan a proactive and preventative approach, much of which will hinge on personalized nutrition.

If all this seems far-fetched and overly futuristic, what if I told you that the early forms of this technology already exist and are being commercialized as we speak?

Personalized Health and Nutrition

Have you ever had a friend who swears by a particular diet only to find you barely shed any pounds when you try it? Or maybe, even worse, the prescribed diet leads you to *gain* weight? How could this be?

The answer to this frustrating and confusing riddle is as simple and as complex as genetics. Our genes play a fundamental role in how the body responds to certain eating habits, meaning different individuals likely have different optimal diets, and a diet plan that helps one person lose weight may not have the same effect for another.

For the last hundred years, "diet" has been viewed largely as something that is optimal for all people. Recent data (and common sense) indicates that different individuals need different diets for optimal health. What this means is that experts should not be giving generalized diet advice. Nutrition recommendations should be based on the genetic factors underlying different people's individual responses to what they eat.

For Dr. Larry Smarr, a hard-core computer scientist, the human body is the computer, and an individual's genome is a person's operating system. Mapping the human genome used to cost millions. Soon the price will drop below $1,000. Once people know their genetic makeup and begin thoroughly monitoring their bodily systems, they will theoretically approach the point where computers can "know" a lot more about them than any doctor ever could. As Larry told me, "In a human body, you have roughly ten times as many DNA cells that are microbes as you do human cells, and you have roughly one hundred times as many genes in the gut as you have in each of your human cells, all of which is outside of medicine and outside of nutrition."

In doing research for this book, I was introduced to a doctor who provides personalized nutrition and health solutions to Manhattan's elite. When I asked if he would be willing to work with me, he literally laughed in my face. "Dude, I mean, I know you have a successful start-up and all, but almost all my clients are literally billionaires." I asked how much his service costs, and I vomited a little bit in my mouth when he responded. He charges over $100,000. Out of pocket. Per year. On a recurring basis.

This doctor appreciated my "poor man" plight and referred me to Health Nucleus, a different service, at a more "reasonable" price point. Health Nucleus is the brainchild of Craig Venter, the biotechnologist who instantly secured his spot as one of the most famous scientists in history when he successfully sequenced the human genome in 2000. When we talk about the dramatic reductions in the cost of human genome mapping, much of this is due to Venter's pioneering work. I wanted to learn more.

Health Nucleus bills itself as "a new clinical research center harnessing recent advancements in genomics—combined with a comprehensive curation of personal health history—to uncover your health risks and serve as the basis for a personalized approach to your health." I reached out to their team and spent an hour on the phone with the Health Nucleus client care coordinator.

He described how Health Nucleus "combines the latest technology in whole genome sequencing with a suite of state-of-the-art health assessments to provide you with a 360-degree view of your personal health." Over an eight-hour visit at their San Diego headquarters, they conduct: a full genome sequencing, "spanning all 6 billion base pairs of DNA"; microbiome sequencing that "quantifies the collective genomes of the microorganisms that live inside and on the human body"; a brain and body MRI scan "for early detection and screening and to provide a baseline for the future"; and a "metabolome characterization which enables us to measure the products of all our biochemical cellular reactions."

Health Nucleus is pretty unabashed in their ambition to use data and technology to transform medicine and make it truly personalized. This feels like the version 1.0 of what Larry envisions. Once they have conducted their eight-hour visit and developed a baseline assessment, Health Nucleus provides you with ongoing health advice to help you understand how new genetic risk associations, medical discoveries, and treatments impact your unique profile. They then work with you and your doctor to develop prevention plans (including nutrition) to solve problems before they even start.

It was the most legitimate approach to personalized nutrition that I had found, and I was excited to schedule my visit. Until I asked about the price:

Twenty-five thousand dollars.

Twenty-five thousand dollars for an eight-hour exam? Really?

And that, in a nutshell, is the reality of personalized nutrition today: It exists, but at a price point that is only affordable for those with a few spare million to burn. Personalized health and nutrition, while increasingly feasible from a technology perspective, is still insanely expensive—at least for mere mortals. I was excited to know that pioneers like Craig Venter were working on problems of this magnitude and complexity, but similar to the journey that supercomputers made from the early 1980s to today's iPhone, both from a cost and feasibility perspective, personalized nutrition has a long way to go before you will find it in the average consumer's pocket.

Dori and the Chamber

I didn't have a spare $100,000 or even a measly $25,000 sitting around under my couch cushions, so I looked for a more reasonably priced alternative to the billionaires' wellness plan. The same doctor whom I mentioned above who provides personalized nutrition and health solutions to Manhattan's elite suggested that I connect with Avigdor Dori Arad, a Ph.D. candidate in nutrition and exercise physiology at Columbia University.

Dori and I hit it off immediately. He is lean, five foot eight, with a shaved head, a thick Israeli accent, and a big smile. Dori was born and raised in Israel and started his career as the commanding officer of a fitness and combat unit within the Israel Defense Forces. From 2005 to 2009, he studied nutrition at UConn while playing Division I soccer, where he eventually won the Big East Most Valuable Player of the year award, in addition to Big East Championships in 2007 and 2009. Prior to starting his Ph.D. at Columbia, Dori returned to Israel to play professional soccer.

As we talked, and as I reflected on what I had learned so far, I came to a realization similar to Larry's: If you want good health, you can't just blindly trust how you feel. Dori invited me to his lab at Saint Luke's Hospital so that I could take my self-exploration to the next level.

Most of Dori's research focuses on metabolism, exercise physiology, and human performance. I wanted to more deeply understand how much and what I should be eating to maintain optimal health, and Dori offered to work with me. We put a plan in place to determine exactly how many calories I needed to consume every day and what type of food I should consume in order to lose weight, gain muscle, and optimize my life as much as possible.

I met Dori up at Columbia one day, and he showed me around his lab. "People can get comfortable with many situations, but they can be in danger," he told me. "For example, you can think your household budget is balancing, but if for twenty years you don't look at your paycheck and you never look at your credit card bill, imagine what could happen. After twenty years, you realize you haven't been making as much money as you thought, but you kept spending—then you wake up and find you are in life-threatening debt.

"The analogy holds true for the body. Most people have no idea how much energy they need or how much they burn. Over the years, we have become more sedentary, and the amount of energy that people now burn has decreased significantly. People think we burn the same amount that we burned on average historically, but that's not true—due to commuting, online shopping, working at a desk— we are now burning much less energy than we did historically. Additionally, we are taking in many more calories than we think because of how food is now produced and prepared."

The same way people have an accountant to help with their personal finances and taxes, Dori recommends that most people work with a nutritionist to help balance their caloric budget. There is too much confusing information today, and people need help.

"There is definitely a lot of nonsense out there," Dori told me, "but there's nothing better than the metabolic chamber for determining what your body actually burns each day."

The metabolic chamber. Even the name sounds scary!

Dori and his team built the chamber from scratch in order to have the most accurate instrument for measuring calorimetry in the world. It is a ten-foot-by-ten-foot sealed-off bariatric chamber (the door is a used submarine hatch!) where Dori's team can monitor oxygen input and carbon dioxide output. With the ability to measure oxygen consumption down to the milliliter per kilogram per second, Dori can tell his patients down to the calorie exactly how much they should be eating in order to maintain, gain, or lose weight.

We sealed the chamber one morning at 8:00 A.M., and I didn't come out until the next morning. I brought in all my own food and fluids. I exercised on a stationary bike. I wrote. And I welcomed the reprieve from the boisterous office and two young kids—it felt a bit like I was on a monk's retreat to the soul of my metabolism!

Following my session in the chamber, Dori provided me with reams of data that I pored over: total energy expenditure, sleep energy expenditure, exercise energy expenditure, my twenty-four-hour respiratory exchange ratio. My fitness and health had never been this quantified before, and as the old MBA axiom goes, if you can't measure it, you can't manage it. I worked with Dori to develop a nutrition plan based off hard data. I finally knew what my body needed to be healthy, and I felt good.

Feast or Future?

Not everyone sees the quantified self in a positive light. Do we actually need to know this much about ourselves to be healthy? Is such an obsession with health even *healthy*? In 1996, a new eating disorder was coined: orthorexia, which literally means a "fixation on righteous eating." Orthorexia starts out as an innocent attempt to eat better.[16] But orthorexics become obsessed with health, purity, and food quality—and spend much of their time and mental energy determining what and how much to eat, and dealing with the consequences when their willpower falls prey to the plate of warm chocolate chip cookies in the kitchen.[17]

At the peak of my quantified self/biohacking/nutrition obsession, I had sent my poop out to a lab to map my microbiome; sent my blood to a lab to perform a food sensitivity test; shipped four additional vials of blood to another lab to track over one hundred blood biomarkers. I had spat in tubes and shipped them across the country to have my DNA genotyped. I was using two different diet-tracking apps and three different fitness platforms on my phone.

And, of course, I had sequestered myself in a metabolic chamber for twenty-four hours.

One night when I was in the depths of my quantified nutrition self-experimentation, I found myself in my kitchen with my new-born second daughter slung over one shoulder. I propped her bottle of breast milk on the window ledge where we have a rocking chair and a view of the Hudson River and the Freedom Tower. It was the last day in June, and the sun was still setting, casting bold orange rays against the symmetrical inverted triangles of the Freedom Tower. It was my wife's first night off from baby duty and she was out with friends, and I was planning to set up shop by the window and watch the sunset while I fed my daughter.

Instead what happened is this: I spent the next forty-five min-utes on my nutrition-tracking app hunched over my kitchen counter, scanning cheese, spinach, and ground chia seeds and inputting other ingredients like eggs, garlic, and kale. By the time I was done jug-gling my daughter and inputting all the ingredients, I turned around to find that it was pitch black outside, and I had missed the sunset.

And then it hit me: This was emblematic of what can happen when food becomes nothing more than nutrition. I could and should have spent the last minutes of the day staring at the sun reflecting off the river and the Western Hemisphere's tallest building. Instead I spent that time looking like Gollum addicted to his precious phone, pecking away, inputting data points to make sure that I was accu-rately tracking myself.

Optimizing happiness, health, and longevity is complex. At this point in human history, we have the capabilities to quantify the self to the extent needed to tailor optimal nutrition, health, and living—but the solutions are cumbersome, expensive, and often end up stripping the healthy joy from life. We will get there soon (within the next decade or two), but for now, the quantified self requires far too much manual input (and obsession) to make it a reality for most people.

So, in the interim, because we don't have the answers, let's not pretend like we do. We all need to do our own research and testing to figure out what blend of nutrition, stress, sleep, and exercise works best for each one of us as individuals. There is no one-size-fits-all approach, there are no shortcuts—and for many of us, being healthy is healthier without having to worry about health.

The fundamental challenge here is that the only bridge to the future is through technology, innovation, and behavior change. These transformations will not come overnight, but due to their initial cost, they will by necessity have to start with the "elite"—folks willing to pay top dollar for life enhancements that at first probably seem ludicrous—think of the $100,000 annual longevity program or the car phone back in the 1980s.

Over time, as the cost curve drops, what were once overpriced technological trinkets will become interwoven with how we all think about day-to-day life. Over the span of thirty years, the car phone evolved from a bauble for narcissistic Wall Street types to the smartphone, which is now used by billions of people around the world. The same evolution will take place over the coming decades for "bioenhancements." Those technologies, services, and products that today are the playthings of billionaires will in a matter of years redefine how we all live our lives.

At a certain point, I found that it's "healthier" to pull back from the brink of obsession and to return to treating food as food and not nutrition. The World Health Organization defines health as an optimal physical, mental, and social state with the absence of disease. As Dori told me after my chamber session, "In the United States today, many people are compromising their health, and the perspective is not 'How do I optimize my health?' but rather 'How do I just survive and make it through the day?' I work with a lot of clinical patients who for many years were not in good health, and when you talk to them about eating well, it looks and feels much different from what they actually do.

"We are in the process of moving from disease-centered to patient-centered medicine, and this means looking at health holistically. Not just 'Does this guy have a problem with his weight?' but also 'Does this guy have the right social support network around him? Does he exhibit tendencies toward depression?' A person is not one dimension, and this is vital to optimizing health."

At Plated, our Second Core Belief is: *The definition of healthy living is intensely personal.* Over the next ten years, we will see an accelerated digital transformation of nutrition and the role it plays within medicine, health care, and social policy more broadly. I am a true believer that food can be either medicine or poison. However, far too many doctors do not start with food and nutrition but rather treat it as an afterthought. This must change, and at Plated, we will help make the change happen.

At Plated, we are building a future where technology (Fitbit, Apple Watch), biomedical and nutritional data collection (23andMe, uBiome), cloud computing, food sourcing and manufacturing, and delivery infrastructure come together to provide a personalized, convenient, and affordable answer to the question "What should I eat?"

In the next and final course, I'll share more about why and how we started Plated, acknowledging that the entire experience that surrounds food is multidimensional, with many opportunities for improvement. We see the future of food, nutrition, and health—and we're building Plated to get there faster.

Picture of an Evolved Eater

Michael Ibrahim, Dorchester, Massachusetts

I started Plated as a life choice to get healthier, and I've been a happy customer for almost four years. I've now lost a total of 130 pounds, and I have Plated to thank for that.

I'm originally from Kentucky of all places, and I moved to Boston for the art scene. Growing up in the South, the food landscape was primarily fast food, or just crap. With no access to fresh food and farmers' markets, you're conditioned to what is fast, easy, and cheap. My parents didn't cook, and I never learned how to cook. This came with me when I became an adult, even in Boston. Before Plated, dinner was pretty terrible. I ate amazingly large quantities of just terrible crap.

After Plated, now I don't even go to the grocery store anymore. People come over, and they look in my cupboards, and there's like one thing of vanilla and some salt and pepper, and they're like, "Do you not eat?" Plated has completely changed how I think about and eat food. I no longer go to the grocery store or order takeout or buy food the "traditional way."

Plated for me was about learning to be fluent in the language of good food, learning how to use olive oil, how to chop veggies, that kind of simple stuff that no one taught me. I can now transcribe that to when I'm out at restaurants, I know how food is prepared and if it's good for me. Plated was an education moment of how to prepare food and become an educated person when it comes to food. Plated is part food discovery and part Julia Child cooking course, and this whole lifelong journey you go on, not to make it sound weird, but I discovered this whole new potential part of my life, and I just needed the tools to unlock it.

When I first tried Plated, weight loss wasn't even on the menu. I was just tired of eating the same three foods, and takeout was really expensive. I used Plated as a springboard to make better life decisions. I've learned that it is much better to have a balanced portion of really amazing-tasting food than two pounds of bland mess. Plated also got me thinking of balancing exercise with good eating, and a Fitbit later,

I'm walking fifteen thousand steps a day. I know that Plated is not a "diet plan," but having portioned, healthy, and fresh food delivered weekly was just what I needed to get me going on my journey. Plated really was the first step in a whole series of life changes and life adjustments for me. Food change led to cutting things out, which led to being more active, which led to enjoying life and being able to live as I had always dreamed of living.

If it wasn't for you guys, I wouldn't have made this change. Plated taught me that life can be better than what I have now.

Third Course

How to Feed Ten Billion People

8

Don't Live on Empty Calories or an Empty Mission

One-liner: From the Marine Corps to Wall Street to taking the entrepreneurial plunge—why we started Plated.

From day one in the Marine Corps, I was steeped in a centuries-old culture that rests on principles of dependability, integrity, decisiveness, unselfishness, courage, and enthusiasm. I would lean on these traits, and the importance of building a strong mission-driven culture to support them, later at Plated. A week after leaving active duty with the Marine Corps in 2011, I started work at Goldman Sachs.

Within a month of my start date, the Occupy Wall Street movement started gaining steam in Zuccotti Park. It was a strange time to be simultaneously working on Wall Street and commanding a platoon of American warriors—I was now a reservist with the Marines, spending one long weekend per month with my unit in Memphis. America had waged over a decade of war, we had reengineered the way the world thought about credit and money, and we had changed over six billion individuals' fashion, eating, and entertainment habits. Suddenly, I found myself working and living at the nexus of the American military and Wall Street, the two forces primarily responsible for the rise of America during the previous century.

From the Desert to the Desk

The decadence on Wall Street was still omnipresent, even after toning things down. Management showered us with perks—complimentary shoes, shorts, heart-rate monitors, spinning classes, yoga studios, saunas, and hot tubs; up to twenty-five dollars in takeout every night you worked past 8:00 P.M.; catered steak lunches—every bell and whistle you could possibly imagine. But I couldn't get beyond one glaring truth: To me, the company was missing its Mission, with a capital *M*.

After coming from the Marine Corps, where *everything* boiled back up to the mission, I felt totally lost. Monday through Friday on Wall Street was a bizarre juxtaposition to my weekends in Memphis with my reserve unit. I would take a flight down from New York City to Tennessee after work, get in around midnight, and then report for duty at 6:00 the next morning. I'd fly back late on Sunday, sleep a few hours, and drag myself down to Wall Street to be at my desk at 7:00 Monday morning.

I was exhausted, and I was depressed. I was logging twelve-hour days boosting marginal basis points for the world's richest people. The lack of mission was killing me; I felt my stress levels increasing as I envisioned the rest of my life unfolding in an Excel model.

Throughout my time on Wall Street, the only mission I found there was making money, which never came remotely close to satisfying my vision for my life. At one point, a senior partner invited me to join a phone call with one of Europe's wealthiest families, discussing the intricacies of buying railroads and German shopping malls out of bankruptcy. That was the most fun and interesting thing that happened while I worked in finance. And it was a ten-minute phone call.

The specter of working this job for the next few years, let alone the rest of my life, bummed me out. I found it incredibly tough to sell something that I didn't fundamentally believe in.

At the same time, admittedly, I certainly wasn't immune to the litany of perks. The lifestyle and corporate culture were seductive, and I could feel the expensive dinners and daily shoeshines gently nudging me away from any pre–Wall Street trajectory.

Sure, the catered steak lunches and takeout dinners were great, but between my diet, my work hours, and my travel to Memphis, post–Marine Corps active duty, I put on over twenty pounds in under six months. I had started to *look* sick. I scarfed down doughnuts and coffee for breakfast, bags of chips and enormous sandwiches for lunch, and greasy pad thai takeout for dinner—all the while sitting at my desk from 7:00 A.M. to 7:00 P.M. Nights when I wasn't eating at work, I went out for drinks and dinner with clients or potential clients. I'd often get home after 10 P.M., crash, wake before sunrise, and start all over again. The bank offered all the free exercise tools and gym equipment you could ask for, but I rarely had the time to use them.

I was fatter, paler, and grumpier, the least optimistic I had ever been in my life. When I looked in the mirror, I felt like my anger and depression were manifesting on the outside. My wife noticed. My mom noticed. Even random people I'd never met noticed. I knew things were bad when, one fall morning, I was walking to work and a homeless man on West Fourteenth Street slapped me on the back and said, "Cheer up, young man!"

The Best Ideas Are Born from Failure

One of the most disheartening parts about working sales on Wall Street was that I was courting the exact kind of people I wanted to be. My job was to track down promising entrepreneurs, get to know them, and then convince them to fork over their hard-earned money. To that end, I was given a credit card and was told to wine and dine dozens of up-and-coming start-up entrepreneurs. That was one major perk of the job: I took my prospective clients to all the best New York City restaurants, places where food existed on an entirely different level from anything I'd experienced before.

By 2011, the farm-to-table movement was really taking off. I was eating out constantly because of my job, and gradually, I began to pay more attention to sourcing. Up to that point, I had never really thought about the food system, how a cow happily roaming the fields becomes a delicious steak sizzling on your plate—I knew so little about the food supply chain that at the time I didn't even realize that the vast majority of American cows no longer roam in fields at all.

But all of a sudden, I saw messaging everywhere that illuminated different parts of that process. The best restaurants made a point of offering locally sourced and sustainably grown ingredients—eggs from happy chickens, grass-fed beef, basil grown on a Brooklyn rooftop. I'd never thought about it before, maybe because it hadn't been brought to my attention, but now that my own awareness around food was growing, I could actually taste the difference. The food tasted better when there was thought behind where it came from and how it was prepared.

The owners and head chefs of these restaurants were top-notch, the sort of people who came around to each table to introduce themselves and do a "quality check" during the meal. They were trained in the art of hospitality, highly skilled at giving each customer a personalized experience. The more restaurateurs and chefs I met, the more I thought about the importance of authenticity, personalization, and transparency in the food industry. These themes would become core to how Josh and I thought about building and scaling Plated.

Every time I took an entrepreneur out to eat, we were 100 percent reliant on the person serving us the food—and not just the restaurant owner but the whole team of people who had played a part in getting that food from farm to table. These were people I would never meet, but I had to implicitly trust them. What were they doing to the food along the way? Was the food safe to begin with?

I also began thinking more critically about what it meant to *eat well*. What did it mean to eat meat versus vegetables? Was it worth paying a premium for good food? What did "good food" even mean?

These thoughts and others were whirling through my head during the nice dinners, where I sat across the table from promising start-up entrepreneurs and realized I wanted to be them. I loved the fact that entrepreneurship was unexplored terrain, far away from the stultifying financial machine of Wall Street or the fixed path of the Marine Corps, where I didn't get any say in my own future. Starting my own business held the tantalizing promise of everything I had longed for—freedom, risk, and adventure. I wanted in.

I needed the money from my job to pay down my student loans, but I was already checked out. And checked-out people rarely make the best choices.

Eventually, as you might expect would happen to a checked-out employee, I was fired. I had failed. Miserably. Three years later, Goldman Sachs would name me one of the world's "100 Most Intriguing Entrepreneurs." But I didn't know that as I trudged up the deserted walkway with the Hudson River sloshing against the embankment. I was freaked out and demoralized and anxious as hell. But I could feel the Goldman handcuffs unlocking and clattering to the ground. I also knew that my future was in no one's hands but my own, and that felt good.

For some of the people I met at Goldman, business was about the full-tilt, relentless pursuit of profits at the expense of everything else—health, happiness, broader society. For me, of course, business was about making money, but in the same way that being human is about making muscle. Yes, we need our bodies to have muscle if we are going to survive. The body needs the anabolic and catabolic processes of metabolism in order to break and build muscle, to layer lean mass onto what is otherwise a brittle and vulnerable skeletal frame. But that second-by-second process that starts with eating and ends with mitochondria is not our mission and source of meaning as human beings. Building muscle is not our mission in life, unless you are a bodybuilder. The process of creating muscle enables us to survive, it allows us to spend our time dreaming, sweating, struggling, and achieving. And the same goes for money—it is a means to accomplish a mission, not the mission in and of itself.

The process of evolution exists to constantly improve and redefine how life should be lived. And that cold winter day in January 2012, I began to evolve and move beyond my earlier definitions of what it meant to live and survive. Making money alone was not enough to satisfy my own evolution, in the same way that making muscle was not enough to sustain my fundamentally human search for meaning.

Yes, making money was a goal. I wanted to pay down my student loans, move out of our shoe box Manhattan apartment, go on vacations, send my kids to college—but it was about so much more than that. I felt compelled to create and contribute and build something bigger than myself. I fantasized about leaving behind the world of shuffling financial instruments in order to make something, or at least to improve something. I wanted to get my fingernails dirty and feel the stress and vigor of transforming an impossible dream into reality. I had the desire to improve people's lives, to make millions of people happier, healthier, and safer—I wanted to make their lives better. That, to me, is what business is supposed to do, and I wanted in.

I had developed a deep respect for the entrepreneurs who left their corporate jobs to build businesses from scratch. I had seen how fashionable it was to romanticize entrepreneurs; my professors at HBS celebrated the geniuses who broke rules to change industries and the world. Politicians praised them as job creators. Tabloids covered the lifestyles of Mark Zuckerberg and Richard Branson. But I saw that the reality of entrepreneurship was as romantic as packing boxes and dirty fingernails.

It was time to take the entrepreneurial plunge.

From Inspiration to Perspiration

I first met Josh when we were only a few months out from graduation at Harvard Business School. A massive earthquake hit Haiti, and a group of us volunteered to help out down there for a couple of weeks. Josh and I worked side by side demolishing houses, handing out water, and consoling folks who had lost everyone and everything in their lives. We slept under mosquito nets on plywood bunk beds, and we stared nervously at one another as the earthquake's aftershocks rumbled through our camp. It was a powerful way to get to know someone and to see how that person operates under stress.

After taking the entrepreneurial plunge, Josh was the first person I turned to. He was one of the smartest, most levelheaded people I knew. He grew up as an air force kid, moving more than a dozen times both domestically and abroad before graduating from high school. He received his engineering degree from Georgia Tech and immediately took his own entrepreneurial plunge. By the time we started chatting about start-up opportunities in early 2012, Josh had built multiple businesses and had even sold one.

We went through a few weeks of "founder dating" and quickly realized that we wanted to build something together. We had very complementary backgrounds (I was loud, bold, and obnoxious; Josh was cool, calm, and collected), and we knew from Haiti that we worked well together, even when times got tough.

We knew we wanted to work on something big, where the mission was as important as the money. We knew starting a business from scratch was going to mean a minimum of five years of heads-down grinding, and we wanted our baby to be something we'd be passionate about for decades to come, not just some flash-in-the-pan faddish app.

We spent weeks batting around different ideas and ultimately fell in love with the food industry. Well, falling in love with the food industry is not exactly accurate. It's more like we began to realize just how broken many parts of the industry are and how much opportunity there was to build a big, valuable business while improving the lives of millions of people.

We saw Chipotle, a mass-market restaurant that for all intents and purposes sold one product (burritos), doing $4 billion in top-line revenue, trading publicly at close to a $20 billion market capitalization. We saw big grocery chains doing tens of billions of dollars in revenue but with very slim EBITDA margins. We saw tens of millions of consumers who expected more, whether it was an escape from food deserts or an elevated yet still affordable dinner experience. And we saw hundreds of billions of dollars in annual food waste. Even though we were young and had no experience in the food industry beyond our preliminary research, we were confident we could build a better business model for food.

When Josh and I started to think through how to build a better food business, we homed in on cooking as the starting point. We knew we wanted to use technology and data in our business model to improve forecasting, reduce waste, and expand profit margins. And through talking to potential customers, what is called customer discovery, we came to realize that there was a massive opportunity to improve one of humanity's most fundamental activities—cooking dinner.

We wanted to build a business that would change how millions and eventually billions of people thought about food, and we realized that the first step to accomplishing this was dinner.

Our first objective was to build a successful product and system for making cooking easier and more personalized and sustainable. Cooking dinner seemed like the hardest piece of the puzzle to solve. If we could solve for this, then over time, we could scale our business beyond dinner. Cooking dinner would be the first lily pad across the pond, and assuming we could make our business model work, it would be just the beginning.

Back in 2012 when we were just getting started, we painted a vision for one another of integrating individualized nutrition data with wearable technology, sourcing locally and sustainably raised ingredients through a world-class, waste-free supply chain, with drone deliveries enabling the perfect food for you and your family exactly where and when you needed it, before you even knew you wanted it. We knew that hundreds of millions of people wanted to eat better, and we wanted to make it easy for them to do so.

In order to reach this lofty vision, we knew we had to get to work.

Big Flavors Start with Small Bites

Starting a business and getting it up and off the ground is a heartbreaking, soul-crushing, mind-expanding labor of contrarian love. To go and start a business in the first place, you have to be a bit nuts. The vast majority of new ventures fail, and to think that you can beat the odds means you need to be extremely confident, extremely naïve, or, more likely, some combination of the two, which was certainly true for both Josh and me.

Choosing the right founding team is the most important part of starting a new business. Strategy, fund-raising, management, marketing—all these things are essential, but if you partner up with the wrong person or people, nothing else matters. The more we talked about cooking food and eating differently, the more Josh and I felt like we had stumbled onto something with real potential.

As we continued to research ideas and conduct customer discovery, we were both burning through our meager personal savings. We cumulatively had over $100,000 of outstanding business school loans and negative personal net worth. We could have walked away from the entrepreneurial dream and found jobs, but we loved working together, and we had an idea that we knew could go the distance.

We wanted to help Americans cook more dinner, with all the health and environmental benefits that this brings. One night I came up with the phrase *Cook More, Live Better*—and we realized that captured what we were trying to do. People want to cook at home—they always have—but it's often just out of reach.

Josh and I thought, what if technology, data, and better logistics could make cooking dinner at home easier and more joyful while reducing the cost and the waste? The fundamentals of the food industry hadn't changed in decades. What if we could create a new and better way to cook dinner? What would we need in order to truly help people Cook More, Live Better?

It seemed like Big Food didn't have the right answers. Yes, they donated millions of dollars to charity, which allowed them to check the corporate social responsibility box, but that didn't hide the fact that they knew they were in trouble and yet still hadn't come up with an adequate solution. They were still using riskily altered ingredients and sourcing food as cheaply as possible and making promises to the American public that they couldn't keep. There were certainly improvements coming from Big Food (better ingredients, fewer chemicals and dyes, more transparent labeling), but the changes were happening around the edges.

The problems with food are so big that they demand disruptive, lateral, courageous, innovative, and maybe even crazy thinking. What if we started from scratch and gave people another option? What if we were the ones who could drive that change?

We already had one of the most important ingredients. Josh was a great engineer. It was in his DNA. His mother is an engineer, too, and he grew up grading calculus papers in the summers to earn extra dollars. He looked at the state of the food system differently—as an engineer. He focused on efficiency, and what he found was really appalling. The food industry is staggeringly large—over $1 trillion a year, second only to health care—and it hasn't changed fundamentally in almost fifty years.

"Sometimes you have inefficient systems that still serve a purpose, like the doorman at a luxury hotel," Josh explained. "But food is this weird case where we have an inefficient system that also doesn't work for people."

After weeks of research and late-night conversations, we were at the point of no return; we either had to part ways and go get jobs, or we had to start a business to solve these problems.

On June 7, 2012, we used LegalZoom to incorporate DineIn-Fresh Inc. from my couch on West Fourteenth Street. We wanted a better name, but we had no money, and after searching GoDaddy for hours, DineInFresh.com was the best thing available. Months later, after we had raised money from investors, we would rebrand and relaunch as Plated.com, but in the early days, it was all about proof of concept, getting a minimum viable product into the market as quickly as humanly possible, for as little money as humanly possible.

It was ninety degrees in Manhattan, which is like two hundred degrees anywhere else, and my air conditioner wasn't really working. We were both sweating profusely. We weren't exactly nervous; it was just really frigging hot on my couch. We bought the domain for $9.99, and we were legit. Sort of. We had a dot-com, a concept, and two heads filled with dreams.

We were going to use technology, data, and better logistics to make it easier for people to Cook More, Live Better, starting with dinner. The idea was born out of three insights:

One

There had to be a better way to eat. We both felt this every day, and millions of Americans were dying from nutrition-related issues.

Two

When we looked at the food industry more broadly, we saw hundreds of billions of dollars in consumption, with no meaningful innovation in decades. The supply chain was inefficient, and up to 40 percent of perishable food went to waste. We figured there had to be a way to use data and technology to get people good, fresh food.

Three

Dinner was the most important meal of the day, yet for many people, including us, the meal didn't live up to expectations, in terms of food or experience. There had to be a way to make dinner better, and we knew cooking would be a part of it.

Nimmi used to come home from her marketing job with a corporate giant to find Josh and me on the couch, strategizing or pounding away at our computers. I had been fired from my job and had spent months searching for my Big Idea. I'm lucky she didn't divorce me.

Instead, she jumped in to help us. She was frustrated with her work, where her job was supposed to be about innovation, but that was challenging to execute at a huge slow-moving company. She said she wanted to go to a start-up, to work with a company that really was innovating, but she knew she couldn't leave her stable job given my risky one. Instead, she started brainstorming with us. "How long should the recipes take?" "Where should we buy the food?" "Who is your target audience?" We had more questions than answers, but we were committed, and we were going for it.

The first steps to getting an idea off the ground are arguably the hardest. This is where most entrepreneurs fail: The idea is good, but the execution doesn't work. As someone famously said, "Life is 1 percent inspiration and 99 percent perspiration."

First order of business: Launch a great website and take the world by storm.

First potential roadblock: I'd never written a line of code in my life.

I had inherited a pretty nasty case of techitis from my mom where I somehow shorted out all electronics within a five-foot radius from me. Despite my handicaps, I taught myself how to code HTML in order to hack together parts of the home page.

Luckily, the company's early web presence did not depend solely on my less-than-awesome web skills. As an engineer who had previously started two software companies, Josh actually knew how to program software. He coded day and night, working with two brothers in Slovakia who barely spoke English, guys we found through a Google search.

While they worked on the web experience, I spent the days hauling myself to the local grocery store on Fourteenth Street and Eighth Avenue, where I'd buy salmon fillets and bunches of basil, hustle them back to my apartment, and pack them into flat-rate FedEx packages. It was super scrappy. I sweated my ass off in the ninety-degree NYC humidity, hauling boxes down to the local shipper and sending them to any friends who were willing to be guinea pigs. (Disclosure: We were begging our friends and family to place an order. Anyone who did was just doing so to be nice and supportive; they were very much sympathy orders.)

If we were going to get DineInFresh off the ground, we were going to need to raise money—that was quickly becoming clear. We had liquidated our 401(k)s, and we were living off our credit cards. The cost of starting a business has come down dramatically since the late 1990s, when it would cost hundreds of thousands of dollars just to get a website live. Through a mix of cloud hosting and out-sourced software and design development, we could afford to pay a few thousand dollars to set up DineInFresh.com as a fully functional e-commerce website.

However, we were planning to ship both bits and bytes *and* bok choy and basil. This would require far more capital. We built rudimentary financial models and forecasted that we would need $200,000 to take us one year. There was just one problem with this: Josh and I were broke.

Selling a Dream Is Hard Work

Our first investor pitch was to my dad. Calling it a pitch is actually a pretty blatant misrepresentation. I took the train out to the sub-urbs where my dad lives, I told him I was not going to be able to pay rent the next month, and I begged him for a loan. He had watched my transitions from the Marine Corps to Wall Street to being an "entrepreneur" with some trepidation. At one point, he staged a mini-intervention of sorts to make sure I wasn't going off the rails. Now I was begging him for money to send perishable food to people via FedEx.

My dad has always been the most supportive person in my life, and this time was no different. He dug into his retirement savings and made the first investment into DineInFresh.com. And while this was an essential infusion to keep our fledgling business alive, in reality, it was only enough to cover rent and the most basic ex-penses of the business.

We continued our fund-raising efforts, and over the next month, we knocked on over 150 doors, trying to raise money, but no one said yes. We were trying to start a consumer-facing e-commerce food business, and neither Josh nor I had ever done anything in con-sumer, e-commerce, or food. It was not an easy sell. And for Josh and me, it was incredibly stressful. We were trying to get the basics of the business off the ground while spending twenty to thirty hours per week pitching people for money. Raising money is a skill, and we needed to become experts at it.

Over the next few months, we made big bets. At one point, both my credit cards were maxed out, I was four months behind on my student loans, and we couldn't pay any of our suppliers. Was it even possible to ship people fresh meat, fish, and produce? Would anyone buy what we were selling?

I soon realized running a start-up in New York City was the adventure of a modern lifetime. For years, I'd been looking for adventures, throwing myself against the world from the Arctic to Indonesia to the Marine Corps and beyond. And here I'd finally found it, staring me in the face from my own laptop in my hometown. There were no more islands left to map and very few mountains left to summit, but the entire Internet was there to be dissected, explored, and mastered. Furthermore, people had needs and problems that were not being answered through traditional business models—and we were going to figure out ways to solve them.

That was our mission. We knew we could use tech and hustle to figure out opportunities and address them. And that's what we did in the early days. Day in and day out, Josh and I found ways to identify problems and build solutions. I had never worked so hard or been so stressed—but I'd also never been as passionate about waking up every day. I had found what I was supposed to do and who I was meant to be. And it felt good.

Everybody Needs a Rabbi

By July of 2012, both our bank accounts were empty, our credit limits were reached, and fund-raising wasn't going well. We were striking out at every turn. We didn't yet have a real product or business, so we were still too early-stage for venture capitalists. Instead, we had approached hundreds of angel investors, wealthy individuals who invest in the earliest stages of start-ups.

Everyone had a different excuse for turning us down. I met the guy who invented the Chipwich ice cream sandwich. "I sold *a billion* Chipwiches!" he screamed at me in the kitchen of his $20 million Park Avenue apartment. "*You think you can sell a billion of these meal things?*" I said yes. He said no. We had hundreds of conversations that ended the same way.

Then a friend from college introduced us to his former boss, Lior Delgo, an Israeli entrepreneur in San Francisco who had just sold his business to Microsoft for over $100 million. I talked with Lior on the phone, and we immediately hit it off. He was former Israeli Special Forces, and we connected over our military backgrounds. Josh and I made a trip to visit Lior and his business partners in Silicon Valley. We brought local grappa and our prototype box, and we spent the weekend at a kid's birthday party, picking fresh lemons in the backyard of a mansion and walking with Lior around the Stanford campus, talking military tactics. After putting my HBS negotiating lessons to work, Lior and his crew ultimately took over a piece of our nascent business in exchange for $400,000 of funding. We gave up a lot, but we gained more—the opportunity to continue. Now we had real money. And it was time to get to work.

We realized pretty quickly that my Manhattan living room was seventy-five degrees on a good day, and Nimmi might actually leave me if we kept hacking and packing raw salmon on our kitchen table. We needed some proper refrigeration. As Josh continued to code, I explored the Bronx, Harlem, Queens, and Brooklyn, looking for cheap refrigerated space. While I found some pretty alarming Bushwick meat lockers, there was nothing acceptable on the market at a reasonable price.

That's when I found Alan "the Rabbi" Dorn on Craigslist. He

was a fifty-year-old Jewish Long Island dad who had pulled himself up by the bootstraps. He had never graduated from high school but had built a bus rental and industrial real estate mini-empire across Queens and northern Brooklyn. Most importantly, he was willing to rent us space in the old Guinness beer-bottling factory on a month-to-month basis. Month-to-month rentals were practically unheard of in NYC, and the rates were more than reasonable. We had ourselves a deal.

We now had enough money to really make stuff happen. We spent that early funding on boxes, building out a refrigerator in the warehouse in Queens, and designing a more functional website and brand. We knew from other start-ups like Bonobos, Warby Parker, and Birchbox that a strong brand with good design would be essential to convincing early adopters to try our service. Josh and I had launched the original website from my couch, but now that we had money, we knew we needed something better. We found what we needed in Hipster Chris, a smart guy from Bushwick with a penchant for cut-off jean shorts and fixed-speed bikes whom we hired to do our brand and website design work.

The three of us—Josh, Hipster Chris, and I—sat in a room together, and over the course of one whiskey-fueled evening, we iterated through dozens of different names and dot-coms. These ranged from the painfully obvious (FoodFresh.com) to the bizarre (Makan .com, inspired by my time in Indonesia). We found a dozen names that we liked, but they were all already in use and not for sale. We were trying to move as quickly as humanly possible, but our domain was worth agonizing over—it was the equivalent of our storefront. If it sounded or looked bad, it would automatically discourage potential customers from giving us a try.

Ultimately, we fell in love with Plated.com. Hipster Chris had some awesome logo ideas around the plate and the dinner table, and we loved the connotations of "plated"—refined, but simple, two syllables, easily pronounceable to the media and customers (unlike

DineInFresh), and reminiscent of memorable dinner experiences. We tracked down the Internet troll who owned the domain, and we structured a special agreement whereby we leased the domain from him over a year, with the right, but not the obligation, to buy the domain outright at the end of twelve months. The thinking here was that we didn't want to spend a massive amount of cash up front on the domain, but that if things were going well (and we'd know that within twelve months), we'd have more cash to buy it. Hence Plated was born.

But we still had a long way to go.

Giving Up Is the Only Sure Way to Fail

The idea to build out a refrigeration system had come from the same source as all great innovation: necessity, also known as, we had no other option. We couldn't afford to rent an actual refrigerated industrial space, so Josh figured out a way for us to build a refrigeration system the low-cost way.

He spent time doing research online and came upon a community of people who were largely hunters and small restaurant owners. These guys built their own refrigerators from air conditioners and after-market adapters. The hunters used them to store their game, and the restaurateurs used them to build affordable walk-in coolers. "This is great!" he said. "We can do this. Let's make it happen."

We put $20,000 of equipment onto our personal credit cards and set out to build a one-thousand-square-foot walk-in refrigerator. We figured we could stuff our little assembly line into the warehouse, pack our boxes, and have our business off and running. As Josh promised, everything would be puppies and roses after that.

Who doesn't want puppies and roses? The big day came. We flipped the system on and waited for the space to cool down. Keep in mind that this was August and the warehouse was a belowground space. The other side of the roof was black asphalt. It was essentially a driveway. That asphalt was absorbing every particle of heat—and it was regularly over ninety degrees outside.

We turned the system on, and Josh went back to the apartment to write code for the website. I stayed out in Queens to watch our baby, making sure it didn't catch fire. It didn't, but that doesn't mean we weren't about to get burned anyway.

One thing we hadn't considered was that this was a system built on retrofitted air-conditioning units. Air-conditioning units drip condensation. We needed to tend to that or our food would soon be swimming. We devised a condensation drainage system that was basically the opposite of sophisticated. The best way to describe it is that I had to empty five-gallon buckets of air conditioner water every six hours. I slept in the warehouse, emptying the buckets while we waited for the room to cool down.

We knew it might take a day or two to stabilize, but we were hopeful. It was a big space, and it took a little while for the concrete to cool and the temperature to come down. I was practically living in the bottling factory, working day and night with a team of contractors to get this contraption to work.

We needed the temperature inside the fridge to be forty degrees. The temperature started out at ninety degrees. After twenty-four hours, it went down to sixty degrees. After two days, it was at fifty-five degrees.

And then it stopped. We couldn't get it any colder. After four horrible days, two things happened:

I got pneumonia and almost died. We realized this was never going to work. Ben Horowitz, a famous tech entrepreneur and legendary venture capitalist, has a term for this sort of experience. He calls it a "WFIO." It stands for *We're Fucked, It's Over.* Hammer to the head of the nail.

After sinking $20,000 and three weeks into the refrigerator, it failed spectacularly. It wasn't nearly cold enough to safely store salmon, beef, and fresh basil. So we swallowed the $20,000 loss on our credit cards (that one hurt), chalked it up to a lesson well learned, and started over.

When It Rains, It Hurricanes

We used the Rabbi's truck to move from Queens to another one of his properties in Brooklyn, a vacant terminal market that dropped into the East River. It was a beautiful location, right on the river, with a panoramic skyline view of Midtown Manhattan. The space had loading docks, and we figured if we couldn't build a refrigerator, we'd rent one. So we called around, I visited a few refrigeration rental places, and eventually I rented a massive, ten-thousand-pound refrigerated cargo container. The guys rented us a Sea Box refrigerated cargo container, which is primarily used on ships to send perishable cargo across the ocean. We put it in the parking lot outside the loading dock, plugged it in to an outlet inside the warehouse, and got going.

On my daily commute, I would ride my bike from my apartment in Manhattan over the Williamsburg Bridge up past the Domino Sugar factory to Greenpoint, where we had our space. At that point, I could fit in my messenger bag all the recipe cards that we'd printed at Kinko's, plus herbs and baguettes from the Whole Foods in Union Square. We pulled our first recipes off the Internet and cobbled together six-step instructions in Microsoft Word. We wouldn't add photos or color to our recipe cards until later.

The Rabbi had connected me to a few people he knew who were looking for full-time warehouse work, and I hired them. One of them still works for us in the Bronx; she is our longest-tenured employee, and over the years, she has been promoted to a leadership position. The Rabbi's contacts were great, but we needed more hands to help.

At this point, we were almost ready for our big launch. We knew we'd need someone who could crush it on social media, and a friend told us about Emily Grant. Emily was living in Atlanta at the time, working as a community manager at an art museum. We interviewed her on Skype and offered her the job shortly thereafter. She started working part-time for us from Atlanta in October. She must have liked us, because she gave her two weeks' notice, leased out her apartment, and got ready to leave for New York.

Amazingly, we convinced *Thrillist* to write about us on the day we were going to launch, and we were super excited about what that could bring. We had delusions of becoming the next big thing overnight. Reporters were going to be banging down our doors.

But a few days before the launch, another story was taking up the airwaves. All the news syndicates were talking about the big storm. *Whatever. It's not going to be a big deal*, we thought. Who knew that we soon would know the wrath of Hurricane Sandy. The day before launch, we stayed up all night making last-minute preparations. We camped out in the warehouse, and as the night went on, the forecast for Hurricane Sandy got worse and worse. No one had slept, but the *Thrillist* piece posted, and we were pumped. We were just waiting for all the sales to roll in.

Our official launch date was October 29, 2012—the day Hurricane Sandy slammed into New York City. By noon, Sandy hit full force. The power went out. We didn't have running water. There was no Internet for miles. Not only was it the worst day of Internet traffic in the history of NYC, our facility came within inches of flooding.

We were basically watching the East River surge into the parking lot, over and over. It picked up our Sea Box—a ten-thousand-pound storage container—and pulled it into the river. The one thing that kept the Sea Box from being washed out and away was a big yellow power cord plugged in inside the warehouse.

We say we were working to get Plated off the ground, but Hurricane Sandy *literally* got Plated off the ground. Imagining that Sea

Box *boing*-ing back and forth like a yo-yo, holding all our time and investments and capital and hopes as it bobbed wildly on the East River, was our next WFIO moment. We almost went out of business before we even opened for business. We were incredibly lucky.

Emily was getting ready to drive herself, her dog, and two bags of clothes up to New York the following week. She called while watching Hurricane Sandy unfold from the sidelines. She had just quit her job and now felt like she was watching her future city literally wash away—and potentially her future company, too. "Oh my God, what is going to happen?" she asked.

Josh knew we had to remain totally calm. "We're in Tribeca," he said. "We're eating homemade ice cream. We're all working out of a friend's apartment today." He told her that we had a little snafu with the shipping container. "But we're good. Everybody's safe. We're fine."

And we were. Over the years, I've met dozens of multimillionaire entrepreneurs and dozens of folks who flopped. To build a business from scratch, you need to be smart and hungry. That's a given. But the biggest difference between success and failure? It's being a stubborn fighter who never quits.

Plated wasn't dead in the water, not quite. But if we were going to make this into a real business, it was time to build the team that would take us there.

Hire People Who Are Smarter Than You

As both Plated and the East Coast recovered from Hurricane Sandy, we realized we needed help getting the word out. Neither Josh nor I had ever done anything remotely related to marketing before, and again, we had no idea how to build a consumer business, or a food business, or an e-commerce business. We started throwing spaghetti against the wall, hoping that something would stick.

It had been two months since launch, and we had not yet figured out how to drive customers, revenue, or traction, and we only had weeks of cash left in our bank accounts.

The practical people in my life began to talk me down from the ledge. I could tell Nimmi thought I was on the brink of losing it, and my mom offered all sorts of consolation, like, "Don't worry, you can always get another job." But I didn't want a job. I wanted Plated to *work*.

We were burning the candle at both ends, trying to find customers to take Plated to the next level, and we were frustrated that we couldn't get any traction. Our product was infinitely better than when we had first started in June. Back then, our beta customers (my mom and dad) would come home to soggy FedEx boxes. But as LinkedIn cofounder Reid Hoffman is fond of saying, if you are not embarrassed by the first version of your product, you've launched too late.

Just a few months later, and we had come a long way. We were working with a part-time recipe editor building world-class recipes, we had a quasi-functional warehouse, and our website was looking like DaBomb Dot-Com, thanks to Hipster Chris. We needed to get the word out, but we had no money to buy advertising or PR or anything besides the bare essentials.

I took the hustle accelerator and put the pedal to the metal. I e-mailed hundreds of journalists, bloggers, and Twitter influencers. I received exactly zero replies. I posted on Facebook, asking my friends for connections to anyone they knew in the media. One of my childhood friends messaged me that she knew the junior tech reporter for *The Wall Street Journal* and that she'd introduce me. I met him at Le Pain Quotidien in Midtown. It was informal—he asked me more questions about my time in the Marines than about Plated. *Well, damn*, I thought after the meeting, thinking it had been a waste and that I'd screwed up the opportunity.

Two hours later, he e-mailed, asking for a photo, saying he would post it on the *WSJ* tech blog *Digits* later in the day. *What?* I thought.

We're getting WSJ *coverage? Yeah!*

The article hit on December 10, 2012, and it really connected with the readers. For the first time *ever*, our customer service phones (a.k.a. our cell phones) started ringing with random people asking to invest. Among them was Andrew McCollum, one of the original Facebook founders. We were weeks away from running out of cash, but Andrew put in money, and we leveraged his name to raise enough money to keep us going.

Now there were big-league investors putting their money behind us. And we were finally getting calls from real customers as opposed to the "sympathy orders" from obliging friends and family.

It felt great, but we were still a tiny operation. Our headquarters was a team of four. We all loved food, and we were decent cooks, but none of us were exactly culinary experts. And since we were positioning Plated as a company that helped people prepare "fantastic gourmet meals" at home, we knew we needed someone whose culinary chops were the crème de la crème. Someone who could make Plated meals not just good, but great.

It turned out the person we needed was Elana Karp. Elana had read about Plated on the *Wall Street Journal* tech blog and thought we were this huge company. She sent an e-mail with her résumé, and when Josh wrote her back, she thought, *The cofounder of Plated e-mailed me! I am such a big deal!*

Elana had graduated from Cornell, done a tour of duty with Teach for America, and then moved to Paris where she spent a year learning to become a classically trained chef. She also worked for a company that started nutritional initiatives in school cafeterias, championing healthy eating and after-school cooking programs in public and private schools around New York City. Her mix of smarts, teaching, and culinary prowess—and her passion for helping people eat better—was exactly what Plated needed. But soon enough, she learned there were just four of us, and she was even more intrigued to be able to start something from scratch. "There's nothing like it—and I want in," she said.

We made many hiring mistakes over the years, but we got something really right when we hired Elana. Josh and I made it our mission to hire only the best people, folks who were smarter than us. Our objective was to make Plated a place where the people were so smart, talented, and awesome that if we applied for a job, we couldn't get hired.

"Plated was the perfect marriage of the things I loved most," Elana says. "That was an awesome moment, when I realized, 'Wow. I can actually make a life and a job and a career out of this thing that brings me so much joy.' Standing on a line in a kitchen is not satisfying to me. But figuring out ways to empower people to cook amazing meals for themselves? That is exciting to me. I started doing private cooking parties where I would travel to people's homes with a knife kit and a bag of groceries and teach them how to cook these amazing meals. Plated allowed me to do this on a massive scale."

With Elana on the team, we were a legit culinary tour de force. We were no longer just a couple of guys chopping salmon alone in our kitchen. We had a culinary cofounder. Over four years later, Elana is part of the Plated bedrock and is the company's chief culinary officer.

9

The Future of Food

One-liner: At Plated, we have a vision for the Future of Food. Our business is about using technology and data to build a better solution for balancing profits, food quality, employee welfare, and sustainability.

I could easily spend another hundred pages telling stories about Plated and how we went from two guys on a couch with an idea to a thriving multi-hundred-million-dollar company serving tens of millions of meals. But that is not this book—to get all the inside baseball on our early and growth trials and tribulations and what we learned along the way, you'll have to wait for volume 2!

This is a book about understanding what happened to food in America to make us sick and unhappy, and how Plated, starting with dinner, will be a driver of the change that must come. How do we go from where we are today to where we want and need to go in the future?

What Plated Figured Out and Why the Model Works

What's so great about our business model? How are we able to work toward our audacious vision while creating a big and profitable business that delights millions of customers each night?

Let's go back to our core beliefs:

Belief 1: Transparency and control over personal and
    planetary health are essential.
Belief 2: The definition of healthy living is intensely personal.
Belief 3: People succeed when it's easier to do the right
    thing than the wrong thing.
Belief 4: Food, and the experiences of choosing it, cooking
    it, and sharing it, are to be celebrated, and thoughtful
    design in all things is an essential part of that celebration.

To build Plated, we knew the food—and the experience of choosing, cooking, and eating it—had to be amazing and personal. That's why Elana was our fourth, and probably still our most important, hire. Elana and the entire culinary team are talented chefs and committed foodies who seek inspiration from their travels, their heritage, their "field trips," and their training. But the Plated business model mixes art and science, using data far more effectively than any traditional recipe creation process.

As Elana says, "Data and technology are integral to our menu creation process and are what, I believe, make it most unique. The Plated culinary creation process is different from most other kitchens in a few ways. First off, we're totally customer obsessed. While we have a strong culinary point of view and house style, we make sure to balance that with the voice of our customers, ensuring we are creating recipes and cooking experience that meet their needs and taste buds."

In order to do that, we need to be nimble. We're constantly testing, revising, and iterating on recipes to make sure that they never get stale. While our menu creation process starts months before a customer orders a recipe, we've set it up in a way that's flexible so that we are able to make changes at any point in the process, which both supports the business and operational needs and the customer's experience. We are sourcing, assembling, and delivering meals to customers in all forty-eight of the Lower 48. What we do behind the scenes is not straightforward.

Elana continues, "Our business model works because we're providing customers with an experience they can't create on their own, and one that has value far beyond the cost of ingredients and delivery. Through our menu choices, we're enabling customers to select and prepare meals they never would have thought of or tried to make at home, and we're exposing them to new ingredients, flavors, and techniques. With each recipe, we're enhancing their dinner experience."

Week after week, it's a challenging task to ensure every customer is presented enough recipe choices to be excited about ordering from our menu. Think about us like a restaurant, where you come back and order a mix of new and encore recipes week after week, for years.

We also gather data and learn how to improve by discovering the implied taste preferences within our customers' observed ordering and eating habits, week after week. By leveraging machine learning applications and artificial intelligence that get smarter without active input from either customers or our own Plated humans, the quality of our menu increases every week. Think about this like Netflix—you can both actively grade the movies and shows you watch, but Netflix also improves their recommendations for you based on passive things you do or don't do, like binge-watching. With Plated, both passive and active customer feedback help us continuously improve, and that is just not possible with your typical nondigitally native food business.

Through our customer order behavior, menu performance, feedback, and ratings, we're able to learn about the success of recipes and menus in ways as specific as individual ingredients and as broad as overall menu mix. This allows us to create menus tailored to our customers in ways far more nuanced than they are even able to ask for. According to Elana, "The challenge—and fun part—for us is to balance this data and technology with the art of our work, and that balance is where the magic happens. It's an exciting process today and one that I think will only get more exciting as we grow. Through our technology and delivery, we're giving customers' time back so they can actually enjoy that dinner experience with the people they love."

Lou Weiss, our former president and CMO, joined us in early 2016 after launching and leading e-commerce for the Vitamin Shoppe. He ultimately ran marketing and merchandising for the retailing giant and helped take them public at a multibillion-dollar valuation.

Lou says, "I joined Plated because Nick and Josh had a vision for the company and the good it could do in the world, and that inspired me, as it does so many of us. But what impressed me most is that they weren't just idealists. They had a business model for successfully achieving their vision. Most food businesses are supply chain driven—whether you're a restaurant or a grocery store, you begin by guessing how much of each ingredient you're going to need, and then you hope like hell that you were right. Since nobody has a crystal ball, the only question is how wrong will you be each day—a little or a lot?"

Lou continues, "Plated's model is the exact opposite—we are driven by the demand chain, not the supply chain. We make our weekly menus available to all our customers five weeks in advance. They look to see what meals we've suggested for them based on their past choices and ratings. Most often, they agree with those choices. Sometimes they swap in a different meal. Sometimes they add an extra night, or extra portions. Sometimes they skip a week. The point is that we know what the consumer demand is *before* we buy our ingredients. There is very little food waste, which is great for both the planet and our bottom line. And the produce is much fresher than the typical supermarket, because we know with a high degree of certainty how much of each ingredient we need each day, and we buy accordingly."

We consider technology and data to be part of our secret sauce, and as any chef knows, you never give away the secret recipe. But at a high level, because we offer so much choice and flexibility, and because we get so many individual meal ratings and reviews, we develop a keen sense of each customer's individual meal preferences. As Lou says, "There isn't a restaurant or grocery store on the planet that knows as much about its customers as we do. And even if they did know what we know, their operations aren't nimble enough to create personal experiences based on that knowledge."

Consumer expectations continue to evolve, and that's not going to change anytime soon. Technology is disrupting everything, both in ways specific to food (like hydroponic agriculture) as well as through innovations like self-driving cars, the quantified-self movement, nutrigenomics, and other technologies that will all affect how food is grown, transported, purchased, and consumed.

When you used to go to the local butcher, they knew the cuts you liked, the quantities you would want, and when you would like it delivered. That personal knowledge and personalization was lost as we moved to supermarkets and large chains. Data analysis with mass customization will bring this back, so that you can be treated to what you want when you want it. Plated, because of our relationship with our consumers and the lack of need to invest in hundreds or thousands of physical retail locations, is in the prime position to leverage these innovations for the benefit of our customers, our business, and the broader supply chain. Our partnership with Albertsons is set to accelerate these exciting innovations at massive scale.

Intelligent Supply Chain

As our first institutional investor, John Frankel from ffVC, says, "The challenge here is this: Can the additional costs of packaging and shipping be offset by not having to hold inventory, not having to rent large footprints in prime locations, and not having to waste as much food? Our bet was that not only would there be offset but that the margins would be strong. The key to doing this was seeing the set of implied logistical and operational challenges being solved as a technology company would through process technology, machine learning, and data visualization, and not as a food manufacturing company might. It is clear to us that Plated is really a technology company that happens to sell food, not a food company that happens to use technology. The technology is not just used within the company but increasingly is being pushed into the supply chain so that the entire system runs more efficiently."

John's bet is paying off. Our intelligent supply chain delivers a superior customer experience with a superior financial profile. What initially attracted John and his investment partners was our approach to the opportunity. "Food is just massive. It's a $1.5 trillion market in the United States. So if you can carve out a few basis points of this market, you have a big business. The key to us was the fact that customers can order what they want, in the quantities they want, to be delivered on the day they want. We knew that this would create a logistical puzzle that many would find challenging to go after, but it also would lead to higher retention and a great business model. We like to invest in those."

The Plated intelligent supply chain is a superior operating model for food sourcing, distribution, and delivery. Dave Allen spent his career building and leading at many of the original Big Food behemoths. He held the most senior operations roles at Frito-Lay, US Foods, and Del Monte. Dave joined the Plated board of directors in 2015.

As Dave says, "I have been in the food business for more than thirty years. The traditional food model requires more time, more waste, and excessive markups for each step in the supply chain. The traditional food supply chain has not implemented effective technology, and both the customer and the business suffer as a consequence. In traditional supply chains, the data is often inaccurate (traditional retail forecast for demand of a specific product is often more than 40 percent inaccurate) and is not shared among the parties; therefore, suppliers keep higher safety stock to meet unexpected demand. This creates excess inventory and waste (spoilage), which is particularly high in produce, seafood, and fresh chicken. Meanwhile, the customer is paying greater than 100 percent retailer markups!

"The Plated model generates superior financial results while providing a convenient, high-quality, healthy, and low-waste option for consumers. That's part of why I decided to invest and join the board. Most importantly, I invested because the team Josh and Nick have built is 'best in class,' and they are fully aligned with the Plated mission of making better food a reality for everyone."

At the end of the day, our customers love us because we enable them to create dinners that match and exceed their expectations— the artistry and the variety that Elana and our culinary team bring to each week's menu and the pride that people feel preparing and sharing these meals with family and friends are the keystone of our success so far. We're obsessed with ensuring that this is true forever—without it, all the innovation in the world doesn't matter.

The Plated Mission Is Bigger Than Plated

Big Food argues that it has allowed humanity to continue our evolution, away from the indentured servitude of the kitchen, and toward a brighter future of convenience and ease, but creating a world of low-effort, high-satiation food as efficiently as possible that's delivered through the traditional retail model has left Big Food in a very tough place. Its product portfolios are dated and increasingly out of sync with how and what consumers want to eat. Despite its best efforts, Big Food's unrelenting need to create the most taste for the lowest possible cost has left it caught in the CRAP Trap.

While some of the Big Food players may break through, the truly innovative solutions are coming from the entrepreneurs drawn to a big problem. The Farmers Business Network in South Dakota and Irving's hydroponic farm in urban New Jersey are emblematic of the hundreds of entrepreneurs who are picking apart each step of the supply chain, searching for the problems and opportunities to use technology to make food better.

When I chat with Irving about the Bowery Farming business model, he practically bubbles over with excitement. "The food system, and particularly fresh produce and the supply chain to support it, has been built around seasonality and the large-scale industrialization of agriculture," he explains. "The cost of these improved efficiencies has meant that both the practices to grow produce and the time for the food to get to your table have been negatively impacted. At Bowery, we are able to change the model fundamentally, not only in terms of the way in which we're growing but also the supply chain itself. We are locating our farms dramatically closer to the point of consumption. We are a hundred times more productive than the same square foot of traditional farmland, and because we are so close to where our food is being consumed, the time from farm to table is a fraction of what industrialized agriculture currently supports."

After building his first company in the enterprise software space, Irving is a big believer in the power and potential of the innovation economy and in entrepreneurs' ability to solve difficult problems. Like Josh and I, Irving wanted to spend his time focusing on a problem that both mattered to him personally and that also mattered to society more broadly. Even a decade ago, the technology that companies like Plated and Bowery Farming have access to today either did not exist or it was not cost effective. To be able to apply cutting-edge technology to a very big problem is incredibly exciting. When we visit Irving at his prototype farm, it feels more like we're going to visit a computer manufacturing facility than an agriculture hub. We don hairnets and clean suits and special booties to keep bacteria out of the system.

"It's the combination of machine automation and a dramatic reduction in the cost of both data and LED lighting systems that makes it possible for Bowery to do what we do today, what wouldn't have been possible ten or even five years ago," explains Irving. "What makes Bowery particularly special is that because there is a heavy reliance on technology, we have thousands of sensors across our farms, measuring millions of points of data, around the environment, and nutritional data, and anything you could think of that affects plant growth, quality, and yield. We can use that information, combined with machine learning and computer vision, to understand what's working and not with how our plants are growing. We can change the variables on a rapid basis that is not possible when you are growing two or three crop cycles per year. Even in our early days, we have already built a much more efficient, effective, and low-cost system overall."

Another serial entrepreneur buddy of mine, Wiley Cerilli, is starting a next-generation food business with the mission of making good food more accessible. Wiley sold his online listing company and became a venture capitalist. He is now building Good Uncle, a delivery-only restaurant that licenses, re-creates, and brings the best dishes from famous restaurants around the world to American college campuses.

As Wiley says, "We're focusing on markets where others are not. Food is becoming a larger and larger part of people's identity and culture, yet most secondary and tertiary markets can be categorically called food deserts, inundated by uninspired and mediocre chains. Good Uncle is the perfect vehicle to bring crave-worthy food with compelling brand stories to markets where nothing of the sort exists. As Howard Morgan, one of the partners at First Round Capital, said, 'This could be a billion-dollar business without ever going to any major city.'"

Another buddy of mine, Matt Corrin, started the Canadian healthy fast casual restaurant chain Freshii. They now have over two hundred stores operating in over twenty countries, and their growth is only accelerating. As Matt says, "My career quickly transitioned from high-end fashion working for the iconic designer Oscar de la Renta to the affordable, fresh-food business working for myself at age twenty-three. I went from dressing runway models to dressing salads. I took a risk and chose to dedicate my career to building a fresh-food empire and changing the way the world eats."

Matt is definitely a big and original thinker. He fervently believes that Freshii will redefine what a restaurant is and will alter people's eating habits. He says, "I believe Freshii will be one of the reasons that life expectancy goes up. Healthy, convenient food will help citizens of the world live longer. In 2015, I wrote an open letter to Steve Easterbrook, the CEO of McDonald's, challenging him to co-brand one of his fourteen thousand Golden Arches locations with one of our Freshii outlets. It shares my vision on what I hope for the future of food:

Imagine a world where every standalone McDonald's, every highway rest stop and campus location offers fresh salad bowls, quinoa, whole grain wraps, and pressed juices—even kids' meals—alongside burgers and Cokes. One outlet can feed the whole family again. Fans of the Big Mac can still indulge while gaining knowledge about fresher, healthier options that taste great and cost no more. I believe this calculated risk would produce a slimmer world and a healthier food industry. To heal hearts and waistlines, we must take action now. Imagine a healthier world. Imagine greater choices for wellness-conscious citizens. Imagine a fast-food industry that is respected and growing again, rather than shunned and shrinking.[1]

Real Food for Real People

We have come a long way in five years, and we are far from finished. There is a lot of money to be made and good to be done in dinner, the Plated way, and our focus now is on getting that model right. We are still decades away from accomplishing our mission to create a world where healthy, affordable, and delicious food is made easy for everyone. I get asked all the time, "How can Plated be for everyone? How are you going to make Plated more affordable?"

I like to respond to this question with an analogy.

When Tesla launched the world's first electric sports car in 2006, their product, the Tesla Roadster, was intentionally designed for the 0.0001 percent—I can practically count on my fingers and toes the number of people who can afford to drop over $100,000 on a sports car with a limited driving radius. But Elon Musk, Tesla cofounder and CEO, was unapologetic: "We're figuring out how to take you to Mars and build a self-sustaining city—to become a truly multi-planetary species."

Wait a second. How do you get from playthings of the über-rich to colonizing Mars?

Answer: The same way you get from twelve-dollar meal kits to feeding ten billion people in a healthy, affordable, delicious, and easy way.

In order to colonize Mars, you need low-cost space travel, you need the ability to harness the sun's energy, and you need a way to store that energy. Following Musk's early success with PayPal, he in quick succession launched or invested in SpaceX (low-cost space travel), SolarCity (the ability to harness the sun's energy), and Tesla (which markets itself as both an automaker and an energy storage company). While the pieces are starting to come together, Musk admits that Mars colonization is probably still twenty to thirty years away. But it's happening.

The one sure way to kill your vision, your mission, and your business is by trying to do too much too soon. For Plated, we need to prove that we can build a big, strong, profitable business that delivers millions of fresh meals across the country. We need profits to do that, and the best way to generate profits as quickly as possible is by starting with dinner (the highest value, most emotional meal of the day), targeting the premium end of the market. That's why Tesla launched with the Roadster, and that's why we launched with twelve-dollar meals. Eventually, we will launch lower-price-point meals that will appeal to everyone, and eventually, that will allow us to feed everyone the way they should be fed. I believe fervently in this. The same way I believe that, eventually, Elon Musk will colonize Mars.

We encourage this type of outlandish, big thinking. We believe in inspiring you and giving you better versions of everything so that you can be a better version of yourself. We want to bring people along for this journey because the definition of a life well lived is intensely personal, and as long as you are continuously raising the bar along the way, we're here to support you. Hell, we'll be here to support you if and when you fall down and fall short, but we just like it more when you're winning!

You don't need to be a ten out of ten. If you're taking steps in the right direction, you're making progress in your personal evolution. I'm much healthier and happier now than I was prior to starting Plated. Do I occasionally want pepperoni pizza and a gallon of India pale ale? Yes! I'm not perfect; I'm far from it. But I take great pride in working on myself every day, and food is a huge part of my own path to becoming an Evolved Eater.

Dinner Is the First Lily Pad

As we scaled the business, we began to think more critically about what it means to be healthy, and we kept returning to the reality that health is more than just managing weight, optimizing body fat, mitigating disease, and maximizing longevity—which is how at least I had conceptualized health for most of my adult life. But as we dug deeper, we arrived at an unexpected place—believing that happiness can help create good health and that cooking makes us happy. And that is reflected in our belief that food is a joy to be celebrated.

Josh says that one of the biggest misconceptions about Plated is that we are only for people who don't want to go to the grocery store or don't know how to cook. As Josh says, "That couldn't be further from the truth! Once customers realize we are saving them from throwing food away at the end of the week, that we're introducing them to a whole new world of flavors and ingredients, and that they're learning new techniques, they usually realize it doesn't matter if they were a professional chef before starting Plated or a total novice!"

As I thought hard about food in my own life and in the process drove myself a bit crazy, I realized something very important: There's no giant authority here; you need to develop your own approach to your own journey to becoming an Evolved Eater.

We built Plated to help. Cooking dinner is the foundation for the first phase of the Plated business model.

10

Cook Your Way to Happiness

One-liner: Cooking is not the panacea for the Flawed American Diet, but it's a good place to start, and it's the foundation for the first phase of the Plated business model.

More Than Anything Else, We Seek Happiness

The future of food and nutrition is coming—but it's not here yet. So what should we do in the interim to maximize our happiness and health? As humans, we believe every other goal—health, beauty, money, or power—is valuable only because we expect that it will make us happy. Happiness is the only major life goal that we seek for its own sake.[1]

Martin Seligman, a one-time president of the American Psychological Association, founded the positive psychology movement and built off earlier fields like humanistic psychology, which emphasized the importance of reaching one's innate potential. Since the 1960s, the study of human happiness has spawned thousands of scholarly articles and hundreds of books—with titles like *The Art of Happiness*, *The Happiness Project*, *The Happiness Animal*, *The Happiness Advantage*, and *Stumbling on Happiness*—many of which focus on increasing well-being and helping people lead more satisfying lives.

So then, as Frank McAndrews writes, "Why aren't we happier? Why have self-reported measures of happiness stayed stagnant for over forty years?"[2]

Part of the problem is that happiness isn't just one thing, and we may actually be biologically hardwired to be dissatisfied most of the time. We all experience different kinds of happiness, but some types of happiness conflict with each other. For example, a happy marriage is something that unfolds and evolves over decades. But successful marriages require a lot of work, and they certainly require sacrificing other forms of happiness—that is, if you find happiness in hanging with friends, going on spontaneous surf trips, and generally being a lazy hedonist. As happiness in one area of life increases, it will often decline in another.[3]

As work has become an increasingly significant portion of our waking hours, spending our leisure time with other hard-charging professionals supports the idea that hard work is part of the good life and that the sacrifices it entails are those that a decent person makes. This is what a group of humans with a strong sense of identity does; we reposition our painful obsessions as potential opportunities—and this is why so many incredibly smart people are some of the least happy people around.[4]

This problem is deepened because humans have evolved to experience happiness in a very short-term and fleeting way. We have all said something like, "I can't wait until (I get that job, I find my life partner, I get that raise, etc.)." We are all also equally guilty of saying something like, "Remember when . . ."

Think about how rarely you hear someone say, "Isn't this *awesome* right now!"

Human society has developed to cope with our brains, which continue to believe that the past and future were and will be better than the present. And there is good reason for why we think this way and believe these things. On the one hand, most humans enjoy a psychological trait called the optimism bias, which leads us to reason that our future will be better than today. On the other hand, most of us also adhere to what psychologists call the Pollyanna principle, which leads us to repress unpleasant information and to remember more vividly pleasurable memories. Depressed people invert these two principles, and they dread the future and regret the past, which makes for a pretty painful present. For most humans, though, the reason that the good old days seem so good is that we focus on the pleasant and forget the pain.[5]

This Pollyanna-optimism deception shines some light on just how short-lived happiness often is. Psychologists who research emotions refer to our addiction to happiness as the hedonic treadmill—human happiness remains stationary, despite our efforts or interventions to advance it.[6] We set our sights on a goal, we work incredibly hard to make it happen, visualizing how achieving the goal will make us happy. But the reality is that after a quick "happiness fix," we quickly revert to our baseline, and we start running after the next thing that we believe will make us happy—the job, the chocolate chip cookie, the girlfriend.

A study of lottery winners and paraplegic accident victims showed that getting what we dream about (winning millions of dollars) rarely makes us happier in the long run. The same psychological mechanism also means that something tragic (like being fully paralyzed in an accident) doesn't make us any unhappier than our baseline, again in the long run. Short term, there is an adaptation period (either up or down), but human psychology is incredibly adaptable.[7]

Entrepreneurs who dream of selling businesses and retiring young often find themselves wondering why they were in such a hurry to sell. After finally raising our first round of venture capital, it was depressing for me to realize how quickly my attitude went from "I'm a real entrepreneur! We raised millions of dollars!" to "I'm an entrepreneur who's only raised single-digit millions."

Before you let this depress you and you throw away all your hopes and dreams, it's important to realize that this is how we were biologically programmed to be from an evolutionary perspective. Focusing on the future is what keeps us motivated to keep advancing humanity, solving the world's biggest problems. Biologically speaking, our ancestors who just sat around in a cloud of ecstasy all day were the ones who got eaten by tigers.

Acknowledging that happiness is a real thing, but that it is fleeting and temporary, should help us enjoy it more fully when it comes into our lives. We should also recognize that it is not possible to be happy across all facets of our lives simultaneously. The Hollywood fiction of "happily ever after" has created a society-wide overdose on outsized expectations.

What is the antidote for unrealistic expectations that lead to being unhappy? People who regularly practice gratitude—by taking time to notice and reflect upon the things they're thankful for—experience more positive emotions and happiness.[8]

And gratitude doesn't need to be reserved only for momentous occasions. Yes, you might express gratitude after receiving a promotion at work, but you can also be thankful for something as simple as cooking a delicious dinner with your family. Research by UC–Davis psychologist Robert Emmons, author of *Thanks!: How the New Science of Gratitude Can Make You Happier*, shows that simply keeping a gratitude journal—regularly writing brief reflections on moments for which we're thankful—can significantly increase well-being and life satisfaction.[9]

But what does any of this have to do with food and cooking? Is cooking actually that important to our health, happiness, and survival? Can cooking possibly help us find a better approach to food and life?

Turns out, it can.

Cook Your Way to Happiness

Josh and I decided to start with cooking because we believe that it is the simplest step we can all take to make ourselves healthier and happier starting today. Cooking is the best way to both connect to where your food is coming from and to ensure that you and your family are eating well. Cooking can both help us fix the Flawed American Diet and make us happier, healthier, and more connected. We are not going to stop with cooking dinner, but it is where we are starting, and it's really important to us and our customers.

What I have found is this: When you fail at food, you fail at life.

Remember Maslow's hierarchy of needs from chapter 1? Ahead of even safety and security, food forms the base of the pyramid. Food is the most fundamental need we have as humans. If you don't figure out food, nothing else matters—not family, friends, sex, self-esteem, confidence, creativity, self-actualization. That's because without a strong food foundation, it is impossible to experience the emotions, ambitions, and relationships that make life worth living.

Foodies, activists, chefs, farmers, and TV personalities have succeeded in making food a part of the mainstream conversation. And this conversation is driving the growth of "new" foods and food sources (farmers' markets, organic food, farm-to-table restaurants) and more information about how to cook (TV and app-based cooking shows, an infinite number of online recipes). But our food culture is slower to change.

From its start, American cooking was characterized by the adjective Americans love most: big. American cooks worked with big pieces of meat and big piles of starch that grossly outweighed the small portions of fruits and vegetables. American cooking was not about cuisine, it was about getting the job done. Across the nineteenth and twentieth centuries, we were moving too fast and trying to accomplish too much—there was just no time to invest in food or cooking culture.

In 1877, Juliet Corson, the head of the New York Cooking School, lamented the wastefulness of American cooks. "In no other land," she wrote, "is there such a profusion of food, and certainly in none is so much wasted from sheer ignorance, and spoiled by bad cooking." A real food culture—that *way* of eating—never evolved into something recognizable, and where it did, it was not preserved. Jean Anthelme Brillat-Savarin, who said, "Tell me what you eat: I will tell you who you are," would have found that difficult to do in early America.[10]

As Dan Barber writes, "With few ingrained food habits, Americans are among the least tradition-bound of food cultures."[11] We mix and match cuisines as we please, picking the best (or worst) from around the world to form atrocities like Denny's Mac 'n Cheese Big Daddy Patty Melt or Rochester's infamous Garbage Plate. This mashup culture has been a blessing in many ways because we are more free to experiment, invent, and test new approaches to everything (jazz, national parks, denim jeans) than anywhere else in the world.

The flip side of this blessing is that our history lacks an ingrained and robust model for good eating. The world's most recognizable cuisines (French, Italian, Chinese, Indian, Turkish) were formed around organizing principles of what was available preindustrialization. In most of these countries, the limited ingredients available to farmers meant that grains or vegetables took center plate, with meat playing the supporting role. Classic dishes like bouillabaisse in French cuisine and paella in Spanish were developed to optimize what the land and sea produced. We never benefited from such a natural system of forced sustainability, and as a consequence, sustainable values don't penetrate our cooking culture. As Dan Barber writes, "Today's chefs create and follow rules that are so flexible they're really more like traffic signals—there to be observed but just as easily ignored."[12]

This flexibility and willingness to innovate and improvise should mean that we have the opportunity to transform American cooking the same way jazz evolved into blues and then rock and then hip-hop over time. The future of American cuisine will represent a paradigm shift, a new way of thinking about cooking and eating that defies the way we eat today.

In looking at the future of American cuisine, we need to go beyond cheekily named chickens and an obsession with kale grown on Brooklyn rooftops. Since the best global cuisines evolved over thousands of years, through a dance with tradition and heartache and burned fingertips and scorched tongues, how do we go about architecting our own American cuisine? How do we go from where we are today to where we need to be in the future if our children are to enjoy the same luxuries we take for granted every night at dinnertime?

**Today the Majority of Calories
Are Consumed Away from Home**

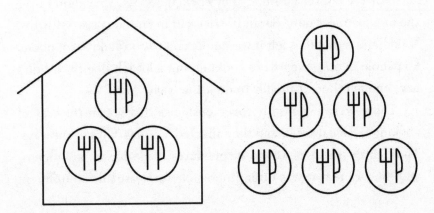

The Joy of Cooking?

For much of my adult life, I was definitely in the "majority of calories consumed away from home" camp—for that matter, I still am.
I'm off to work early, I eat breakfast and lunch at my desk, and I try
to make it home for dinner. I'm clearly not the only one.

People *know* and *say* that they want to spend more time cooking
and eating at home, but there is a profound disconnect between how
people *say* they want to eat and how they actually do it. We dug into
more research on eating out versus eating in and found that people
did want to cook more—they just didn't always have the time,
knowledge, confidence, or resources to do so. And that was often
true across socioeconomic lines.

Take the recent academic article "The Joy of Cooking?" Sociol-
ogists Sarah Bowen, Sinikka Elliott, and Joslyn Brenton spent eighteen months following nearly two hundred low- and middle-income
moms, logging hundreds of hours interviewing and observing how
these moms fed their families. What they found was surprising:
Many of the moms *did* enjoy cooking—and in fact cooked for their
families several days a week. But time and budget constraints made
it hard for these moms to make home-cooked meals the way they
wanted.[13]

"For the poorer families, they cooked because they didn't have
the money to eat out," Sarah Bowen said in an interview with *Vox*.
"Middle-class families felt it was important to cook and eat at home.
So people in our study were cooking, but a lot felt like they didn't
have enough time or money to do it the 'right' way."[14]

There were essentially three obstacles that got in the way of
cooking the ideal meal, and they affected families in different ways.
Those three obstacles were time pressures, trade-offs to save money,
and the fact that it was often impossible to please all the different

family members. Kids are notoriously picky (I know because I have a couple of munchkins at home).

For the low-income families, time pressure was a big deal. They often had unpredictable schedules and jobs that kept them out late, including service industry positions where they might miss the dinner hour altogether. And while the middle-income moms had more predictable work schedules, they still talked about not having enough time to make a home-cooked meal with everyone in the family flying in from different directions and converging in the kitchen around six o'clock.

Bowen talks about "one mom who was going to community college and commuting back and forth by bus." This woman and her kids would get home around 8:00 P.M. every day—way too late to then start planning and preparing a meal. The woman, who struggled financially, felt that if she could just get home a couple of hours earlier, maybe she could cook like she wanted to. She *liked* cooking. She had grown up with a grandmother who loved to cook, and she felt it was an important way to show her kids she cared. But it just wasn't possible with her schedule.

Many of us can relate to the "time pressure" challenges of cooking. On the nights I work late, the last thing I want to do after getting home at 9:00, 10:00, or 11:00 P.M. is make a meal. Prior to starting Plated, I hadn't been very kind to my body, and while I wasn't struggling with obesity or diabetes, in some ways, that was just luck of the draw; plenty of people in my family were suffering from both.

As a nation, we are spending less time in the kitchen than ever. In 1965, the average middle-class American cooked for ninety-eight minutes a day. By 2007, that number had declined to fifty-five minutes.[15] About 20 percent of our calories come from restaurants and fast-food establishments, compared with just 6 percent in 1977.[16] Since 1970, the number of fast-food joints in the United States has more than doubled.[17] In 1960, 13 percent of Americans were obese, compared with 35 percent today.[18] The kitchen has been replaced with a recipe for disaster.

And who could blame us for trading the hot stove for the drive-through window? Critics of the home-cooking movement charge that it's antifeminist (because women still cook the majority of the time) and elitist (*you* try searing tuna with avocado and ponzu while holding down two jobs and shopping with food stamps). Home cooking, concluded Amanda Marcotte in a 2014 *Slate* article, is "expensive and time-consuming, and often done for a bunch of ingrates who would rather just be eating fast food anyway."[19]

But the more research we did, the more the *what* and *how* of what we were eating as a society didn't match up with the ways we claimed to want to eat. There was a huge gap that demanded to be filled, and until we filled it, millions of people were dying every year from diseases that could be prevented if we changed our eating habits.

But changing habits is *hard*. Again, most folks viscerally and intellectually understand that they should be eating better. However, it is going from *understanding* to *implementation* where everything falls apart. "Sure, I'd like a piece of wild-caught salmon over seared lacinato kale, but that's not going to happen when I'm rushing home to get my kid from day care after working ten hours."

So first, we had to solve the cooking conundrum.

Cook More, Live Better

There are three main benefits to cooking: wellness, happiness, and connection or mindfulness. I'll briefly go through all three now.

Wellness. As Michael Pollan said, "The most important thing you can do for your kids' long-term health is to teach them to cook. The best diet is: Eat anything you want as long as you cook it yourself."[20] Research suggests that Pollan is onto something.

A 2014 Johns Hopkins study found people who frequently cook meals at home eat healthier and consume fewer calories than those who cook less. Participants who cooked dinner six or seven times a week consumed 6 percent fewer calories and 12 percent fewer grams of sugar than those who cooked no more than once a week. The study also suggests that those who frequently cooked at home also consumed fewer calories on the occasions when they ate out. "When people cook most of their meals at home, they consume fewer carbohydrates, less sugar, and less fat than those who cook less or not at all—even if they are not trying to lose weight," says Julia A. Wolfson, a fellow at the Johns Hopkins Center for a Livable Future and lead author of the study.[21]

Researchers surveyed Canadian fifth graders about how much they liked certain foods. The study found that "those who reported helping with meal preparation at home showed a 10 percent stronger preference for vegetables than their peers who didn't help cook."[22]

"Obesity is an escalating public health problem that contributes to other serious health issues, including diabetes, high blood pressure, and heart disease," says Wolfson. "The evidence shows people who cook at home eat a more healthy diet. Moving forward, it's important to educate the public about the benefits of cooking at home, and to identify strategies that encourage and enable more cooking at home."

Happiness. "Not cooking is a big mistake," Mark Bittman warned in a 2014 piece in *Time.* "And it's one that's costing us money, good times, control, serenity, and, yes, vastly better health."[23] Involving ourselves in cooking a meal connects us with the complex supply chain that raises and delivers our food, which in turn makes us more active, engaged, and generally better consumers.

Additionally, cooking is a natural and easy excuse to spend time in proximity with the person or people we love most. Research shows that happiness is directly correlated to time spent with friends and family engaging in constructive projects together, like cooking. A recent study in *The American Journal of Clinical Nutrition* demonstrates how cooking at home actually makes us happier than eating fancy meals out at a restaurant.[24]

The study looked at how food choices influence mood. One hundred and sixty women reported what they ate for ten days. They were contacted every two hours to report what they had recently eaten and how they were feeling after. The researchers looked at two aspects of each meal: whether it was eaten at home or out (restaurants, fast food, cafés, etc.) and whether the meal was healthier than the woman's "baseline" or typical meal, or more indulgent / less healthy.

Most people (except for those who live in Manhattan and use their oven as a shoe rack) think that eating out is special. But this study found that women were significantly happier and less stressed after eating at home and after eating healthier meals. As the authors conclude, "The home is a privileged environment that nurtures healthy eating and in which healthier food choices trigger more positive emotions."[25]

Connection or Mindfulness. We have become disconnected from the visceral experience of *making stuff*. Most Americans now spend their days in office buildings behind computer screens, pounding out e-mails, not pounding out the production of physical goods that made America a global force in the mid-twentieth century. Many of us may not produce anything tangible and directly applicable to our lives *ever*.

After I started cooking, two things happened:

First, I started paying attention to where my ingredients were coming from. The more I cooked, the more labels I looked at in an attempt to understand where my food was coming from, what was in it, and how it would impact me when I ate it. Experiencing ingredients firsthand went a long way toward helping me understand the importance of standards. Understanding where food comes from helped me become a more active and engaged eater. As I learned to cook, it inspired a sense of mindfulness that went beyond the kitchen, extending to being present and aware of how I interacted with others and the earth. I also started meditating and doing yoga. But in case you fear that I was veering toward the edge of some new age hippie revelation, I still shot machine guns on the weekend with the Marines to balance it all out.

Second, my confidence in the kitchen skyrocketed. I found myself capable of putting together foods in a way that had previously seemed like magic. This was empowering, and I got a major self-esteem boost out of it, both inside and outside the kitchen.

We conducted a poll of Plated employees and customers to see whether this experience expanded beyond just me. We asked, "After learning to cook, do you feel more confident?" For folks who claimed that they "rarely or never cooked" before starting to cook with Plated, over 80 percent of people responded that they agreed or strongly agreed.

So if cooking is a key enabler of our wellness, happiness, connectedness, and confidence, then why is there not more concerted effort to make cooking a bigger part of the modern American lifestyle?

Back to the Future

For me, cooking has been transformative. In the vast majority of the world, including the United States, women do the majority of household activities—including cooking. On an average day in the

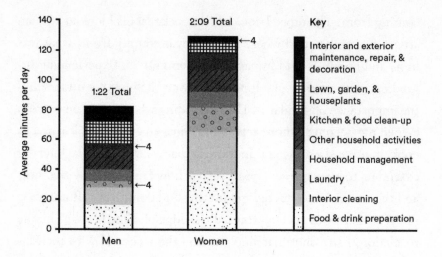

United States, women spend more than twice as much time as men preparing food.[26] As I learned how to cook through Plated, I became the primary "food preparer" in our house—I wouldn't go so far as to call myself a chef. While I may not contribute as much as my wife would like to laundry, cleaning, and interior decorating, I get away with it because I am the one who makes sure our kids are fed.

Multiple people's lives directly depend on me showing up and literally putting food on the table. In the Marine Corps, as officers, we were taught that we ate last—if there was only enough food to feed the guys, then we would go hungry. Similarly, at Plated, there were times in the early years when Josh and I went without salaries for months on end so that we could afford to make payroll and feed our people. At home, while I have had the good fortune of never going hungry, I have embraced what it means to serve.

When we outsource all our food needs to someone else, even if that someone else knows more about baking or sautéing or nutrition or bicycle delivery than we do, we lose something more important than time. We lose our connection to our food and the earth that grows it. The future of healthy, affordable, and delicious food is in the hands of the humans who live in the dirt (or hydroponics) and abide by its rules, conjuring the alchemy that transforms seeds into feasts. Physically preparing a meal connects us with the agricultural systems that produce our food, making us more active and engaged consumers.

Some may claim that ignorance is bliss, but I'd argue that sticking your head in the sand like a free-range ostrich is no way to eat or live. We owe it to ourselves and to our children to become more educated and concerned about what food means, how it works, and who is involved.

When we outsource all our food needs to someone else, we also lose our connection to the people around us who make us happy. In a 2013 appearance by Louis C.K., the comedian explains why he doesn't want to get a cell phone for his kids: because constant attachment to a screen deadens your experience of the world. "You never feel completely sad or completely happy, you just feel . . . kinda satisfied with your products. And then you die."

Nights when I am home on time, I read a book (or five) to my daughters before bed. One of my older daughter's favorites is *The Velveteen Rabbit*. At one point, the rabbit asks the Skin Horse if it hurts to be "real."

" 'Sometimes,' said the Skin Horse, for he was always truthful. 'When you are Real you don't mind being hurt.' "

This children's narrative took me to the same place that Louis C.K. was going—that being "real" means being uncomfortable at times. It means you ask tough questions, and one consequence is that you might find answers that make you feel upset.

One of the most important questions of our time is how much truth we are willing to trade for comfort. This is the age-old CRAP Trap circling back once again.

Technology exists to make our lives safer, healthier, easier, and more comfortable. We are building a new economy based on technology-driven convenience, and it makes sense that this convenience at all costs has bled over into other areas of our lives. Dating based on a swipe comes with a lot less friction than marriages that require a lifetime of work.

But what if removing friction and increasing comfort isn't the right goal? As our expectations continue to climb—photoshopped social profiles, on-demand everything—what are the implications for our food, our reality, and our happiness? What if, like a stormy ocean that makes stones smooth and beautiful by knocking them together, the point of being human is to bump up against each other, burn our fingers a bit, and confront the truth in order to become better and more beautiful?[27] This may be less convenient and more painful and uncomfortable in the short term, but over the long run, it will make us happier, and at the end of the day, that is what we all want above everything else.

Conclusion

New Food Ideas Require New Food Companies

Building a Better Way to Eat

In a recent interview, one consumer packaged goods (CPG) executive admitted, "We're kind of fucked." One-third of American consumers surveyed by Deloitte, a consultancy, said they would pay at least 10 percent more for the "craft" version of a good, a greater percentage than would pay extra for convenience or innovation. Interest in organic products has been a particular challenge for big manufacturers whose riskily altered products include such mouth-moistening ingredients as sodium benzoate and Yellow 6. EY, another consultancy, recently surveyed CPG executives. Eighty percent didn't believe their company could adapt to customer demand. Kristina Rogers, global head of consumer products and retail at EY, posits that Big Food "may need to rethink their business from scratch, not just trim costs and sign deals to acquire promising young brands."[1]

Big Food is not going to feed ten billion people the way they need to be fed—in a healthy, affordable, real, fresh, delicious, and convenient way. Nearly twice as much money is spent on processed foods and sweets today as compared to a few decades ago. As food industry veteran Hank Cardello told me, "The traditional food industry is very efficient if you want something convenient that tastes half-decent. However, it is horribly efficient for nutritious foods that are fresh. And it's nearly impossible for them to change."[2]

We can't look to Big Food to solve our food problems. When I spoke with Marion Nestle (no relation to the food company Nestlé), the Paulette Goddard Professor of Nutrition, Food Studies, and Public Health at New York University and the author of *What to Eat*, I asked her, "How do you feel about the current state of Big Food?" Her response was priceless. "Poor things. They're doing so badly."[3]

As I spoke with hundreds of people who had spent their lives devoted to studying, producing, and fixing food, I was happy to learn that the general mood about the future of food was positive. The combination of changing consumer attitudes and behavior, convenience-enabling technology, media interest, consumer education, and market forces has folks feeling generally optimistic, except for one thing: making the solution happen fast enough.

When I spoke with Pulitzer Prize–winning food reporter Michael Moss, he told me, "The food giants think their ace in the hole for winning and maintaining their dominance of the food system is population growth and the ten billion people that we'll have by 2050. This has the companies convinced that we will come running to them for calories, no matter how low quality those calories are, because they are the ones who will feed the world, not just the small portion of the world who can afford to eat better."[4]

Big Food doesn't have the answers, and it is not capable of developing the answers on its own. This is where Plated and the new breed of food companies come in. If we are going to feed the world, and do it affordably, conveniently, and in a sustainable, healthy, and delicious way, then the answer must come from technology and data-driven companies like Plated. We can prove that great food can be grown in a good way, affordably, where workers are treated well and where the earth, our waistlines, our wallets, and our relationships don't pay the price.

We can't think about changing only parts of the way we eat; that is too shortsighted and narrow-minded. Over time, we will need to build an entirely new and better way to eat.[5]

From Idea to Action

The Big Food insiders, journalists, and academics I spoke with have written widely and thoughtfully about the food problems we face in America today. They come at these problems from different angles, but I couldn't help but notice they were united in one common theme: They all expressed a certain level of frustration. They could see the problems, but they couldn't necessarily do anything about them. They were like Cassandra from the Greek myth, foretelling the future in vain.

Many of these experts are not executors and operators. They are living in journalistic, scientific, and academic realms. They do *not* live in the realm of smashing your head repeatedly against a wall, also known as building a business. Don't get me wrong—they deeply feel and understand the problems surrounding food in the modern world—as do millions of other people, but they are fairly limited in what they can actually *do* about it. So they publish excellent books and clear-eyed blog posts, articles, and thought pieces that slowly change the conversation toward what they all hope to be a better solution.

When I asked Marion Nestle how we should help people eat better, she said, "You just make healthy food and talk about how good it tastes. You don't do anything else. I think it's that simple. You don't hit people over the head with how healthy certain foods are. You just talk about how good and convenient they are.

"I don't think people need products. People need food. The real problem is with people not knowing how to cook or feeling inadequate about their cooking skills, or feeling like it takes an enormous amount of time and effort after a long day at work when they just don't want to bother. I imagine that's the problem you're trying to solve."

Yes! That is exactly the problem we are solving. Of course, making all the seemingly simple pieces work together in harmony to *deliver* that solution is surprisingly hard. Trust me—we've spent the last five years working to get the seemingly simple pieces to work together to deliver tens of millions of healthy, affordable, and delicious meals across America. It's really hard and takes a very talented and committed team of people to make it work.

We are not the only folks using data and technology to reimagine how food is produced, distributed, and delivered. Our category is on fire. Some of the biggest and most respected institutions on Wall Street have put out research predicting that our category could grow by more than thirty-five times over the next ten years![6]

This is because our business model is not just incrementally but dramatically better than that of Big Food. We are better for customers, better for the environment, better for employees, and better for investors. But you don't have to take my word for it; *Forbes* recently reported that spending at grocery stores decreases by over 7 percent for folks who use a "meal kit."[7]

Plated is a great service that can help you get close to your food, close to your family, and closer to the way you want to live, but it's not all or nothing—we're not talking about going back to the farm to churn your own butter.

We have found that when folks cook with us two nights per week, they experience the benefits of connection, happiness, and wellness. Just getting started with Plated is taking a big step in the right direction.

As Josh says, "People should expect Plated to get better and better at two things. First, we're going to continue to expand the types of meals we offer (think breakfasts, lunches, appetizers, and others) as part of our mission to make it easy to eat well. Essentially, making it easier to get good food that you *want*. The second thing to look out for, over time, is that we'll get better at understanding what you *need*, specifically from a health and nutrition perspective, and building that automatically into the delicious recommendations we make to you as a customer. Nutrition science is a young, dynamic, and exciting field, and we're excited to help advance the science as much as we can."

New food ideas, new food solutions, and a new food reality require new food companies like Plated, but we are not going to accomplish our mission on our own. There is a monumental amount of work to be done if we are going to feed ten billion people in a healthy, affordable, and delicious way.

And we need your help.

Here are four ways you can help:

1. **Join us at Plated!**
2. **Tell politicians what you think.**
3. **Teach the kids in your life how to cook.**
4. **Recognize that you have massive power.**

1. Join us at Plated!

We are always hiring, looking for the hungry, smart, and mission-driven folks who want to commit their skills and energy to solving big, tough problems. **Visit us at Plated.com/careers and drop us a line!**

We are also building a coalition of like-minded companies and institutions. If you lead a business or team and believe that we can work together to accomplish our mission of helping people eat more real, fresh, delicious food, we would love to hear from you!

2.   Tell politicians what you think.

As I sit writing this conclusion, the state of politics in this country is more contentious and gridlocked than at any time in recent memory. That doesn't mean we should turn our backs on politics and the making of policy. To the contrary, now more than ever, we need to speak up and make our voices heard where laws and policies are made.

There are two main areas where you can help by telling politicians what you think:

   a. **Limit government subsidies for bad behaviors.**
   b. **Fight dietary inequality and increase access to fresh, real foods.**

Limit government subsidies for bad behaviors

Many of the government regulations that were designed to protect us from the dangers inherent in the industrial food system are not relevant in a more transparent, regional food system. These rules discriminate against smaller businesses because the costs of complying with the paperwork requirements cannot be spread out over a large volume of food sales. Small vendors are at a disadvantage because they must pass those costs on to consumers, making their food more expensive than the mass-produced variety. These burdensome regulations also discourage entrepreneurs from starting up in the first place.

Getting people to fall in love and get hooked on real food is the answer to moving away from inexpensive, unhealthy food. That starts with getting people excited about real food and where it comes from. And that in turn starts with farmers growing veggies instead of soy and corn. Massive monocrop farms are increasingly becoming the norm as consolidation of smaller family-owned farms (like my family's) continues. But diversified multicrop and multianimal farms do not receive government subsidies.

The government's calorie-maximizing policies, a holdover from the Great Depression, no longer make sense in a country more troubled by obesity than by hunger. In its push for large monocultures, the USDA prohibited farms that receive grain subsidies from growing fruits and vegetables. This puts the government in the insane position of subsidizing the cost of fast food while actively prohibiting more farms from growing fruits and vegetables.[8]

Subsidies and government cleanup measures are not included in the price you pay for riskily altered products, but if they were, good food would not seem so expensive in comparison. The production, processing, and marketing of riskily altered provisions creates collateral damage (like obesity, diabetes, and environmental "dead zones") that taxpayers are on the hook to fix. Consider the Twenty-nine Palms–sized area in the Gulf of Mexico now known as a "dead zone" because nothing can survive in the oxygen-starved water, a result of manure and pesticide runoff. Who pays for the cleanup? We do. Who pays to address antibiotic-resistant strains of bacteria caused by the overuse of antibiotics on factory farms? We do. Who pays to treat people with type 2 diabetes, which they get from consuming the riskily altered products that are sold cheaply because the companies making them get subsidies? We do.

Tell your politicians that these policies are insane and that you're fed up.

Visit us at Plated.com/PlatedPolicy to figure out how to help.

Fight dietary inequality and increase access to fresh, real foods

The societal problem with riskily altered food products costing less than fresh fruits and veggies is that the poor cannot afford to deal with the health problems that come from eating hyperprocessed foods in massive quantities. Why does fresh, nutritious, responsibly grown food only need to be for the rich? High-quality, fresh, real food should be the right of every American. If we are going to fix the food problem in this country, increasing access to nutritious affordable food has to be a part of the solution.

While according to the Mayo Clinic, only 2.7 percent of Americans have a "healthy lifestyle," for wealthy folks, diets are improving. A recent study tracking changes in eating habits between 1999 and 2012 suggests that Americans are eating more whole fruits, nuts, and seeds and drinking fewer sodas. But the study also revealed that the gap between the diets of the wealthy and the poor is widening.[9]

This news shouldn't come as a revelation. Low-income places are less likely to have full-service grocery stores or farmers' markets, let alone bountiful shelves of organic produce. Lower-income folks often have no car, so they have to shop at the sort of bodegas and convenience stores that offer Cheetos, Lunchables, and Mountain Dew rather than fresh produce. In Newark, New Jersey, just a few miles as the crow flies from where I live, Renée Fuller, an elderly woman who walks with a cane, has to go to the next town, West Orange, to shop for food. "You want a banana, you have to travel.

There's not many supermarkets. There's nothing convenient . . . You have bodegas and corner stores that sell cold cuts and sandwiches, but not many vegetables . . . I get my food stamps once a month. I can't stock up on fruits for the whole month."[10]

Poor urban areas that are at least a mile from the nearest supermarket, and rural areas that are at least ten miles from any grocery store, are considered food deserts. According to the USDA, nearly half of the 23.5 million people living in areas deemed food deserts also qualify as low income. They also suffer from higher-than-average rates of diet-related illness, and they spend a higher percentage of their limited time and resources than the rest of Americans traveling to buy food.[11]

So what can you do about this?

Here's one idea: We need to make it possible to use food stamps online. We need to reinvent food stamps for this new digital era.

Of people who live in poverty, only 30 percent have access to a car, while 74 percent have access to the Internet. But currently food stamps can't be used on the Internet—which is insane.

Tell your politicians that SNAP should be usable online.

Visit us at Plated.com/SNAP to figure out how to help.

3.   Teach the kids in your life how to cook.

When I was in middle school, several times per week, I had a class on home economics where we learned woodworking, budgeting, sewing, and other basic household skills—like cooking.

You don't hear much about home ec these days, and in fact, the idea of teaching these skills is frowned on by many as a throwback to an earlier time when women's primary occupation was to "keep the house." But the demise of home economics is responsible for a large part of our disconnection from our kitchens, cooking, and our food more broadly. Teenage girls and boys used to learn how to be mindful and capable of cooking.

Unfortunately, these one to two hours per week were co-opted by society for other priorities: teaching teenagers how to avoid pregnancy, say no to drugs, and get a job, instead of how to prepare a meal. Kids lost touch with food, where it comes from, and how to prepare it affordably and efficiently. And this set up tens of millions of us to be reliant on riskily altered products in place of fresh, nutritious, homemade food.

So how can you fight back?

Well, let's assume that home economics isn't going to magically reappear on middle and high school schedules.

That means it's on *you* to teach the kids in your life how to cook and appreciate food. Which leads us to the fourth way that you can help . . .

4.   Recognize that you have massive power.

It's important to recognize that as consumers, we have an enormous amount of power. To prove this point, you need look no further than the mighty McDonald's decision to transition to cage-free eggs by 2025. "We're trying to respond to what our consumers' expectations are today of us and their food supply," says Marion Gross, senior vice president and chief supply chain officer of McDonald's North America. "Consumers are changing. It's about how we evolve to meet those changing customer expectations. We can't remain static and remain relevant to customers."[12]

As consumers, we have the power to change how the food system works, but this means making conscious decisions and prioritizing standards and quality over the cheapest, most convenient product available. And that's why it is okay to be not just unashamed but proud about paying more for good food.

We have talked in depth already about why good, nutritious food is almost always more expensive than the riskily altered products generated by the industrial food system. People who care deeply about food and are willing to pay more for it are often branded snobs or elitists—which leads to hand-wringing and moral angst.[13]

Where does this guilt come from?

We feel guilty about paying more for good food when others are starving, when millions of people around the world and in this country literally beg, borrow, and steal just to eat something. But instead of cringing and crying about this at fancy cocktail parties while the issue persists and we cede ground to those who claim that feeding ten billion requires the perpetuation of industrialized hyperprocessed food, let's directly confront why paying more for good food makes sense for almost everyone.

First, let's start with an axiom: Higher quality stuff is worth more money. Better food tastes better, looks better, and is safer. I call CRAP Consumable Riskily Altered Provisions for a reason—if you eat nutrient-stripped, chemically altered, antibiotic-infused food, you are engaging in risky behavior. As someone's grandma once said, you can either pay your grocer or your doctor. When you short your grocer (and yourself), you end up paying your doctor tenfold over the long run. But what if you don't have the cash on hand to pay for more expensive food in the short term?

That brings us to point two: Eating fresh, unprocessed foods is the best way to reduce your food budget. A pile of kale or a pint of chickpeas costs the same as a single bag of Cheetos. Cooking can move us away from riskily altered provisions, which are more expensive, less healthy, and less emotionally rewarding. Cooking is not hard, but like any skill, it needs to be learned, cultivated, and practiced—and that takes time.

Third, there is more than enough money. We as a society have just decided not to spend it on high-quality food. Think about the amount of money spent on dietary supplements, designer clothes, video games, casinos, and luxury cars. The United States spends more on their cats and dogs than the entire continent of Africa spends on medical care for humans.

Modern humanity has become conditioned to "learned helplessness." This is an actual psychiatric condition where people have been beaten into believing that they have no control over the outcomes in their lives, so they look to others to solve their problems. We need to quit being victims and bring about change ourselves, whether that be in the kitchen, at work, or in our relationships. If you took the average American shopping cart in the checkout line and tossed out all the riskily altered provisions and substituted fresh food, our country would be richer, healthier, and happier.

If advocating for such behavior change makes me an elitist, then that is a pretty depressing referendum on what we value as a society. Let's not disparage positive decision making and attempts to change behavior for the better. I saw what was happening in Iraq and Afghanistan, and I wanted to be a part of the solution, so I joined the Marine Corps. I was thirty pounds overweight after two kids and long hours starting our business, so I signed up for an Ironman triathlon. I saw the food system was broken, and I started a business to fix it.

We can all do better. This is the attitude that keeps humanity moving forward. If we can find money for gadgets, designer clothes, and vacations, we must be able to find the money to improve the quality of the food we eat. Our passions make us human. Cultivating a passion for good food will ultimately make us healthier, happier, and wealthier—at both an individual level and as a society.

It is crucial that we change our attitude toward food. The tobacco industry offers a useful example. As we learned that smoking caused cancer and killed, smoking became less socially acceptable, and in turn, smoking rates have declined. If people could come to view devouring Cheetos or liters of Mountain Dew in the same way, both our waistlines and our medical bills would shrink. Over one-third of American adults are not just overweight but obese. Obesity and the preventable chronic diseases that go with it cost the United States hundreds of billions of dollars in lost GDP every year. I believe the psychological and social toll is even higher. But nutrition is rarely if ever tracked in most health care systems.

Getting our food problem fixed should be a top national priority—for all of us.

Afterword

While I was in South Dakota on my family's farm, after Ron showed me his organic garden, Dawn told me she was annoyed that Ron had planted a row of swiss chard but he had no idea what to do with it and was thinking about giving it all away to his church group. I told him that I loved swiss chard and that I would come up with a recipe that we could eat alongside our steaks.

I Googled "swiss chard recipe," and while five years ago I wouldn't have even known where to start, I now had the confidence to take the cheesy swiss chard recipe I found online, use it as a base, and improvise with the handful of ingredients that were available in the farmhouse cupboard and refrigerator. We used the chard and some freshly pulled onions and garlic from the garden. Dawn works at the local dairy, and instead of using grated Parm, as prescribed, we used a half cup of local Colby cheese that Dawn had made by hand just a few hours earlier.

It was a pretty empowering experience to teach farmers how to cook something that they had grown and produced themselves, and pulled from the earth just minutes before. There is no way I could've done that prior to my journey with Plated.

After dinner, Dawn served fresh whole milk from the dairy that hadn't even been pasteurized yet, alongside a plateful of her irresistible chocolate chip cookies. Instead of obsessing about the cookies and losing my focus on the conversation about our sprawling family tree, I let myself go, and I indulged.

After dinner and dessert, I set off for a four-mile run around the section with the setting sun. Thanks to my time in the metabolic chamber quantifying my own metabolism, I knew that thirty minutes of running hard would burn off those cookies. I had figured out a system that worked for me.

I also took a one-gallon Ziploc bag with me, and on my run, I stopped by Ron's winter wheat trucks and filled up the bag with freshly reaped grains to bring home to mill, ferment, and bake bread from scratch.

I thought about how far we had come, the challenges we had already overcome, and all the challenges we still had ahead of us. We were up against some of the biggest problems that defined the modern world. As I ran down the dirt road that my family had been farming and managing for over a century, with the sun setting against the rustling corn, I felt strong and confident that we would succeed, no matter what the world threw against us.

Notes

Introduction: Toward a Better Food Future

1 Chase Purdy, " 'Nature is not good to human beings': The Chairman of the World's Biggest Food Company Makes the Case for a New Kind of Diet," Quartz, December 27, 2016, http://qz.com/856541/the-worlds-biggest-food-company-makes-the-case-for-its-avant-garde-human-diet/.

2 "A Life Less Sweet: Nestlé Looks for Ways to Boost Stale Growth as Consumers Snub Unhealthy Food," Economist, January 7, 2017.

3 Michael Pollan, Food Rules: An Eater's Manual (New York: Penguin, 2009).

4 "Bitter Fruits: As Incomes Become More Unequal, So Too May the Rate of Healthy Eating," Economist, August 13, 2016, http://www.economist.com/news/united-states/21704801-incomes-become-more-unequal-so-too-may-rate-healthy-eating-bitter-fruits?frsc=dg%7Cc.

5 In his October 2016 New York Times Magazine article, "Big Food Strikes Back," Michael Pollan does a fantastic job of describing the relationships that make up the monolith oftentimes described as "Big Food" in the media.

6 In his book The Third Plate, chef Dan Barber explores in much more detail how the farm-to-table movement came to be and what his philosophy and approach are for making food more sustainable.

7 "21 Reasons Why Plated Changed My Life," Spoon University, December 7, 2016.

1: Our Food Is Killing Us

1 Centers for Disease Control and Prevention, CDC, February 6, 2015: http://www.cdc.gov/nchs/fastats/leading-causes-of-death.htm (accessed March 17, 2015).

2 American Journal of Public Health, "The Impact of Obesity on U.S. Mortality Levels: The Importance of Age and Cohort Factors in Population Estimates," *American Journal of Public Health* 103, no. 10 (2013): 1895–1901.

3 *Fed Up*, directed by Stephanie Soechtig, produced by Atlas Films, 2014.

4 *Overweight and Obesity*, September 9, 2014: http://www.cdc.gov/obesity/data/adult.html (accessed March 19, 2015).

5 J. Cawley and C. Meyerhoefer, *Journal of Health Economics* 31, no. 1 (January 2012): 219–30.

6 I. Lee et al., "Effect of Physical Inactivity on Major Non-Communicable Diseases Worldwide: An Analysis of Burden of Disease and Life Expectancy," *Lancet* 380, no. 9839 (2012): 219–29.

7 "Beyond Willpower: Diet Quality and Quantity Matter," Harvard School of Public Health, http://www.hsph.harvard.edu/obesity-prevention-source/obesity-causes/diet-and-weight/.

8 Dan Barber, *The Third Plate: Field Notes on the Future of Food* (New York: Penguin, 2014), Kindle edition, 11.

9 Wendell Berry, *The Unsettling of America* (San Francisco: Sierra Club Books, 1996).

10 Luke Runyon, "Are Farmers Market Sales Peaking? That Might Be Good for Farmers," NPR, February 5, 2015, http://www.npr.org/sections/thesalt/2015/02/05/384058943/are-farmer-market-sales-peaking-that-might-be-good-for-farmers.

11 "The State of the Specialty Food Industry 2015," Denise Purcell, Specialty Food Association, https://www.specialtyfood.com/news/article/state-specialty-food-industry-2015/.

2: Eating Evolution, Part 1: Cooking Made Us Human

1 Yuval Noah Harari, *Sapiens: A Brief History of Humankind* (New York: HarperCollins, 2015), Kindle edition, 11.

2 Kenneth Miller, "Archaeologists Find Earliest Evidence of Humans Cooking with Fire," *Discover*, May 2013, http://discovermagazine.com/2013/may/09-archaeologists-find-earliest-evidence-of-humans-cooking-with-fire.

3 Steven R. James, "Hominid Use of Fire in the Lower and Middle Pleistocene: A Review of the Evidence," *Current Anthropology* 30, no. 1 (February 1989): 1–26.

4 Richard Wrangham, *Catching Fire: How Cooking Made Us Human* (New York: Basic Books, 2009).

5 Ann Gibbons, "Food for Thought: Did the First Cooked Meals Help Fuel the Dramatic Evolutionary Expansion of the Human Brain?" *Science* 316, no. 5831 (2007): 558–60.

6   Ann Gibbons, "Raw Food Not Enough to Feed Big Brains," *ScienceNow*, American Association for the Advancement of Science, retrieved October 23, 2012.

7   Wrangham, *Catching Fire*.

8   Harari, *Sapiens*, 40.

9   Laura Biel, "Ancient Famine-Fighting Genes Can't Explain Obesity," *ScienceNews*, September 5, 2014, https://www.sciencenews.org/article /ancient-famine-fighting-genes-cant-explain-obesity.

10 S. H. Ahmed, K. Guillem, and Y. Vandaele, "Sugar Addiction: Pushing the Drug-Sugar Analogy to the Limit," *Current Opinion in Clinical Nutrition and Metabolic Care* 16, no. 4 (July 2013): 434–9, doi:10.1097/MCO.0b013e328361c8b8.

11 Harari, *Sapiens*, 48.

12 Ibid., 48–9.

13 Nicholas G. Blurton Jones et al., "Antiquity of Postreproductive Life: Are There Modern Impacts on Hunter-Gatherer Postreproductive Life Spans?" *American Journal of Human Biology* 14 (2002): 184–205.

14 Richard B. Lee and Richard Daly, eds., *The Cambridge Encyclopedia of Hunters and Gatherers* (Cambridge, UK: Cambridge University Press, 1999).

15 Louis Binford, "Human Ancestors: Changing Views of Their Behavior," *Journal of Anthropological Archaeology* 3 (1986): 235–57.

16 M. Sahlins, "Notes on the Original Affluent Society" in *Man the Hunter*, edited by R. B. Lee and I. DeVore (New York: Aldine Publishing Company, 1968), 85–9.

17 Harari, *Sapiens*, 78.

18 Ibid.

19 Ibid.

20 Jared Diamond, *Guns, Germs, and Steel: The Fates of Human Societies* (New York: W. W. Norton, 1997).

21 Ibid.

22 Sean Carroll, "Tracking the Ancestry of Corn Back 9,000 Years," *New York Times*, May 24, 2010.

23 Ibid.

24 Ibid.

25 Harari, *Sapiens*, 82.

26 Ibid.

27 Ibid., 85.

28 Alain Bideau, Bertrand Desjardins, and Hector Perez-Brignoli, eds., *Infant and Child Mortality in the Past* (Oxford, UK: Clarendon Press, 1997); Edward Anthony Wrigley et al., *English Population History from Family Reconstitution, 1580–1837* (Cambridge, UK: Cambridge University Press, 1997), 295–6, 303.

29 Harari, *Sapiens*, 88.

3: Eating Evolution, Part 2: The Birth of Big Food

1 Michael Pollan, "Big Food Strikes Back," *New York Times Magazine*, October 5, 2016.

2 Ibid.

3 Ibid.

4 "Food Processing's Top 100," Food Processing, http://www.foodprocessing.com/top100/top-100-2015/.

5 When comparing PepsiCo 2014 revenue to gross domestic product against "List of Countries by GDP (Nominal)," *Wikipedia*, https://en.wikipedia.org/wiki/List_of_countries_by_GDP_(nominal).

6 Derek Thompson, "Food Is Cheap," *Atlantic*, April 5, 2012, http://www.theatlantic.com/business/archive/2012/04/food-is-cheap/255516/.

7 United Nations Food and Agriculture Organization, 2009 report.

8 T. Colin Campbell and Thomas M. Campbell, *The China Study* (Dallas: BenBella Books, 2016).

9 Kim Bhasin, "15 Facts About Coca-Cola That Will Blow Your Mind," *Business Insider*, June 9, 2011, http://www.businessinsider.com/facts-about-coca-cola-2011-6?op=1.

10 While a majority of women did not work outside the home in the early twentieth century, a significant minority did (some estimates as high as 40 percent), especially those women from low-income and immigrant communities. Their families needed two incomes in order to survive.

11 Michael Pollan, *Cooked*, Netflix documentary series, 2016, https://www.netflix.com/title/80022456.

12 PBS *Frontline*, "Fat."

13 Some experts have gone so far as to preach that Big Food is as guilty as Big Tobacco. Kelly Brownell, a Yale University professor of public health, says, "As a culture, we've become upset by the tobacco companies advertising to children, but we sit idly by while the food companies do the very same thing. And we could make a claim that the toll taken on the public health by a poor diet rivals that taken by tobacco."

14 Michael Carolan, *The Real Cost of Cheap Food* (London: Earthscan, 2011), 74.

15 Pollan, *Cooked*.

16 Tom Philpott, "What the USDA Doesn't Want You to Know About Antibiotics and Factory Farms," *Mother Jones*, July 29, 2011.

17 Thompson, "Food Is Cheap."

18 Barber, *The Third Plate*, 9.

4: "City Boy Goes Country"—Farming and Food Production

1 "Giants in the Earth," SparkNotes, http://www.sparknotes.com/lit
   /giants/context.html.

2 "Corn Palace," Wikipedia, https://en.wikipedia.org/wiki/Corn_Palace.

3 Andrew F. Smith, "Farm Subsidies, Duties, Quotas, and Tariffs," *The Oxford Encyclopedia of Food and Drink in America*, http://www.oxfordreference
   .com.ezproxy.cul.columbia.edu/view/10.1093/acref/9780195154375
   .001.0001/acref-9780195154375-e-0294?rskey=TEB1hc&result=272.

4 "Agricultural Policies Versus Health Policies," Physicians Committee for
   Responsible Medicine, http://www.pcrm.org/health/reports/agriculture
   -and-health-policies-ag-versus-health.

5 Harari, *Sapiens*, 101.

6 AgFunder's AgTech Investing Report (2015), https://research01.agfunder
   .com/2015/AgFunder-AgTech-Investing-Report-2015.pdf.

7 Beth Kowitt, "Can Monsanto Save the Planet?" *Fortune*, June 6, 2016,
   http://fortune.com/monsanto-fortune-500-gmo-foods.

8 "Factory Fresh," *Economist*, June 9, 2016, http://www.economist.com
   /technology-quarterly/2016-06-09/factory-fresh.

9 "David Hula Makes Record 532 Bushels Per Acre to Top NCGA Yield
   Contest," Southeast Farm Press, December 18, 2015, http://south
   eastfarmpress.com/grains/david-hula-makes-record-532-bushels-acre
   -top-ncga-yield-contest.

10 The FBN data gets interesting when you have a whole bunch of farmers
    who are FBN members around you. You can see on your soil types what
    your potential yield could be by looking in a database for all the farmers
    who are growing on a similar soil type with the same seeds and chemicals.
    They can say, "Hey, the average yield for Pioneer P1151, a particular vari-
    ety of corn, is so many bushels per acre, and by the way, you also have
    75 percent of this particular field with the same soil type, so take a look at
    that particular seed variety, and here's the average yield that we're seeing."
    It's a way for farmers to uncover performance information for their
    products where they can realize 11–12 percent yield increases by simply
    optimizing what they're already doing. For the average farmer, this trans-
    lates into $25,000 in savings per year, just on seeds.

5: The CRAP Trap

1 Annual Report to the Nation on the Status of Cancer, 1975–2014, http://
   www.cancer.gov/research/progress/annual-report-nation (accessed May 30,
   2017).

2 "Agricultural Policies Versus Health Policies," Physicians Committee for Responsible Medicine.

3 George A. Bray, Samara Joy Nielsen, and Barry M. Popkin, "Consumption of High-Fructose Corn Syrup in Beverages May Play a Role in the Epidemic of Obesity," *American Journal of Clinical Nutrition* 79, no. 4 (2004): 537–43.

4 Ibid.

5 Michael Moss, *Salt Sugar Fat: How the Food Giants Hooked Us* (New York: Random House Publishing Group, 2013), Kindle Edition, locations 367–70.

6 Lindsay H. Allen and Andrew Prentice, *Encyclopedia of Human Nutrition*, 3rd edition (Cambridge, MA: Academic Press, 2012), 231–33.

7 Moss, *Salt Sugar Fat*, locations 379–81.

8 Ibid., locations 383–90.

9 Ibid., locations 687–95.

10 Ibid., locations 2678–86.

11 Ibid., locations 2692–701.

12 "Changes in Consumption of Omega-3 and Omega-6 Fatty Acids in the United States During the 20th Century," *American Journal of Clinical Nutrition* 93, no. 5 (2011): 950–62.

13 In 1993, a scientist named Adam Drewnowski examined the problem of bingeing, or compulsive overeating. Drewnowski knew there were links between sugar and addiction to opiates; studies showed, for instance, that sweets sometimes eased the pain of heroin withdrawal. So he treated his subjects as if they were drug addicts. He gave them a drug that counters the effect of opiates. This drug, naloxone, is given to people who overdose. Drewnowski offered his subjects a variety of snacks—ranging from popcorn, which was low in sugar, to chocolate chip cookies, which were loaded with sugar, as well as fat. His findings: The drug worked best in curbing the appeal of the snacks that were highest in both. Drewnowski published his study "Invisible Fats" in 1990, and it showed that fat was a double-barrel shotgun when wielded by Big Food.

14 Moss, *Salt Sugar Fat*, locations 2883–8.

6: The Cacophony of Confusion

1 Dr. Yoni Freedhoff, "What's a Food Industry to Do?" YouTube presentation: www.youtube.com/watch?v=-BdFkK-HufU

2 Michael Pollan, "Altered State," *New York Times*, May 3, 2015.

3 Bruce Bradley, "My Story," Bruce Bradley's website, http://brucebradley .com/my-story/.

4   Bruce Bradley, e-mail correspondence with author, September 12, 2016.

5   Bruce Bradley, "Marketing to Kids: Collateral Damage in Big Food's Profit Hunt," Bruce Bradley's website, http://brucebradley.com/food/marketing -to-kids-collateral-damage-in-big-foods-profit-hunt/.

6   Brook Barnes and Brian Stetler, "Nickelodeon Resists Critics of Food Ads," *New York Times*, June 19, 2013, http://www.nytimes.com/2013/06/19 /business/media/nickelodeon-resists-critics-of-food-ads.html?_r =0.

7   Committee on Food Marketing and the Diets of Children and Youth, *Food Marketing to Children and Youth: Threat or Opportunity* (Washington, D.C.: National Academies Press, 2006).

8   Institute of Medicine, *Food Marketing to Children: Threat or Opportunity?* (Washington, D.C.: National Academies Press, 2006).

9   "Food Marketing to Kids," Public Health Law Center, http://public healthlawcenter.org/topics/healthy-eating/food-marketing-kids.

10 "Food Marketing: Presentations for Download," UCONN Rudd Center for Food Policy and Obesity, http://www.uconnruddcenter.org/food -marketing-presentations-for-download.

11 Jennifer L. Harris et al., *Evaluating the Nutrition Quality and Marketing of Children's Cereals* (New Haven, CT: Rudd Center for Food Policy and Obesity, 2009).

12 "Cereal FACTS 2012: A Spoonful of Progress in a Bowl Full of Unhealthy Marketing to Kids," *Yale News*, June 22, 2012, http://news.yale.edu/2012 /06/22/cereal-facts-2012-spoonful-progress-bowl-full-unhealthy -marketing-kids.

13 Emily York, "McDonald's to Kids: Eat Fruit, Drink Milk, Visit Arches," *Chicago Tribune*, March 5, 2012.

14 "Advertising Spending," Cereal FACTS.

15 Elaine Wong, "Frito-Lay Names CMO," *Adweek*, October 5, 2009, http:// www.adweek.com/news/advertising-branding/frito-lay-names-cmo -100547.

16 Michael Mudd, "How to Force Ethics on the Food Industry," *New York Times*, March 13, 2013, http://www.nytimes.com/2013/03/17/opinion /sunday/how-to-force-ethics-on-the-food-industry.html?_r=0.

17 Eric Lipton, "Rival Industries Sweet-Talk the Public," *New York Times*, February 12, 2014, http://www.nytimes.com/2014/02/12/business/rival -industries-sweet-talk-the-public.html?_r=0.

18 Mark Morgan Ford, "The Food Pyramid Turned Upside-Down," Early to Rise, http://www.earlytorise.com/the-food-pyramid-turned-upside-down/.

19 Ibid.

20 "A Fatally Flawed Food Guide," Luise Light, Whale, http://whale.to/a /light.html.

21　Carole Davis and Etta Saltos, "Dietary Recommendations and How They Have Changed Over Time" in *America's Eating Habits: Changes and Consequences*, edited by Elizabeth Frazão (Washington, D.C.: U.S. Department of Agriculture Economic Research Service, 1999), 35, http://www.ers .usda.gov/publications/aib-agricultural-information-bulletin/aib750 .aspx.

22　"Harvard School of Public Health: Food Pyramids," Matzner Clinic, http://www.matznerclinic.com/PDFs/HarvardPyramids.pdf.

23　Gary Taubes, *Good Calories, Bad Calories* (New York: Knopf Doubleday, 2007), Kindle edition, locations 207–11.

24　Davis and Saltos, "Dietary Recommendations," 36.

25　David Perlmutter, *Grain Brain: The Surprising Truth about Wheat, Carbs, and Sugar—Your Brain's Silent Killers* (Boston: Little, Brown , 2013), Kindle edition, 82.

26　Ibid., 82–3.

27　Ibid.

28　Ibid., 83.

29　Jill Carroll, "The Government's Food Pyramid Correlates to Obesity, Critics Say," *Wall Street Journal*, June 13, 2002; "A Fatally Flawed Food Guide," Light.

30　"A Fatally Flawed Food Guide," Light.

31　Ibid.

7: When Food Becomes Nutrition

1　Institute for Integrative Nutrition, e-mail to the author, April 29, 2016.

2　"Unscientific Beliefs about Scientific Topics in Nutrition" held April 27, 2014, at the ASN Scientific Sessions and Annual Meeting at Experimental Biology 2014 in San Diego, California. The symposium was sponsored by the American Society for Nutrition (ASN) and the ASN Nutritional Sciences Council.

3　Andrew Brown, "Let Industry Fund Science," Slate, September 21, 2016, http://www.slate.com/articles/health_and_science/science/2016/09 /should_researchers_have_to_disclose_funding.html.

4　M. B. Cope and D. B. Allison, "White Hat Bias: Examples of its Presence in Obesity Research and a Call for Renewed Commitment to Faithfulness in Research Reporting," *International Journal of Obesity* 34, no. 1 (2010): 84– 88, http://doi.org/10.1038/ijo.2009.239.

5　Gary Taubes, "Do We Really Know What Makes Us Healthy?" *New York Times Magazine*, September 16, 2007.

6 At the center of the Big Fat About-Face is the science of epidemiology it-self. "Establishing the dangers of cholesterol in our blood and the benefits of low-fat diets has always been portrayed as a struggle between science and corporate interests," writes Gary Taubes in *Good Calories, Bad Calories.* "And although it's true that corporate interests have been potent forces in the public debates over the definition of a healthy diet, the essence of the diet-heart controversy has always been scientific."

7 Jonathan D. Schoenfeld and John P. A. Ioannidis, "Is Everything We Eat Associated with Cancer? A Systematic Cookbook Review," *American Journal of Clinical Nutrition* 97, no. 1 (2013): 127–34, http://ajcn.nutrition.org/content/97/1/127.long.

8 Taubes, "Do We Really Know What Makes Us Healthy?"

9 S. Claiborne Johnston et al., "Effect of a US National Institutes of Health programme of Clinical Trials on Public Health and Costs," *Lancet* 367, no. 9519 (2006): 1319–27.

10 Taubes, "Do We Really Know What Makes Us Healthy?"

11 Nina Teicholz, *The Big Fat Surprise: Why Butter, Meat, and Cheese Belong in a Healthy Diet* (New York: Simon & Schuster, 2015), 3.

12 Mark Bowden, "The Measured Man," *Atlantic,* July/August 2012, http://www.theatlantic.com/magazine/archive/2012/07/the-measured-man/309018/.

13 Larry Smarr, phone interview with the author, June 17, 2016.

14 L. Smarr, "Quantifying Your Body: A How-To Guide from a Systems Biology Perspective," *Biotechnology Journal* 7, no. 8 (2012): 980–91.

15 Bowden, "The Measured Man."

16 "Orthorexia Nervosa," Karin Kratina, NEDA, https://www.nationaleatingdisorders.org/orthorexia-nervosa.

17 "Frankly, I'd rather go river rafting," says Dr. H. Gilbert Welch, a profes-sor of medicine at the Dartmouth Institute for Health Policy and Clinical Practice and the author of *Overdiagnosed: Making People Sick in the Pursuit of Health.* "Data is not information. Information is not knowledge. And knowledge is certainly not wisdom." Welch believes that individuals who monitor themselves too closely are pretty much guaranteed to find some-thing "wrong." "It brings to mind the fad a few years ago with getting full-body CT scans," Welch says. "Something like 80 percent of those who did it found something abnormal about themselves. The essence of life is variabil-ity. Constant monitoring is a recipe for all of us to be judged 'sick.' Judging ourselves sick, we seek intervention." Welch rails against current forms of intervention, which today normally starts with drugs or surgery and is rarely risk-free. As Welch sees it, "Arming ourselves with more data is guaranteed to unleash a lot of intervention" on people who are basically healthy. Until

"intervention" starts with nutrition instead of pills or the scalpel, quantification may lead to more harm than good.

9: The Future of Food

1　To read Matt's open letter to the CEO of McDonald's, please go here: https://www.freshii.com/static/pdf/Open_Letter_to_McDonalds.pdf

10: Cook Your Way to Happiness

1　Mihaly Csikszentmihalyi, *Flow: The Psychology of Optimal Experience* (New York: HarperCollins Publishers, 2008).

2　Frank T. McAndrew, "It's Healthier to Be Sad Sometimes Than Happy All the Time," Quartz, October 12, 2016, http://qz.com/760582/we-arent -meant-to-be-happy-all-the-time-and-thats-a-good-thing/.

3　Jennifer Hecht writes on this concept at length in her book *The Happiness Myth*, http://www.jennifermichaelhecht.com/the-happiness-myth/.

4　Joe Pinsker, "Why So Many Smart People Aren't Happy," *Atlantic*, April 26, 2016, http://www.theatlantic.com/business/archive/2016/04/why-so -many-smart-people-arent-happy/479832/.

5　McAndrew, "It's Healthier to Be Sad."

6　"Hedonic Treadmill," Shane Frederick, Yale University, http://faculty .som.yale.edu/ShaneFrederick/HedonicTreadmill.pdf.

7　"Lottery Winners and Accident Victims: Is Happiness Relative?" Philip Brickman, Dan Coates, and Ronnie Janoff-Bulman, UC–San Diego, http://pages.ucsd.edu/~nchristenfeld/Happiness_Readings_files /Class%203%20-%20Brickman%201978.pdf.

8　Derrick Carpenter, "The Science Behind Gratitude (and How It Can Change Your Life)," *Happify Daily*, http://www.happify.com/hd/the -science-behind-gratitude/.

9　Robert Emmons, "Why Gratitude is Good," *Greater Good*, November 16, 2010, http://greatergood.berkeley.edu/article/item/why_gratitude_is_good/.

10　Barber, *The Third Plate*, 16.

11　Ibid.

12　Ibid., 16–17.

13　Sarah Bowen, Sinikka Elliott, and Joslyn Brenton, "The Joy of Cooking?" *Contexts* 13, no. 3 (Summer 2014): 20–25.

14　Sarah Kliff, "The Problem with Home-Cooked Meals," *Vox*, Febru-

ary 11, 2015, http://www.vox.com/2014/9/26/6849169/the-problem
-with-home-cooked-meals.

15 "Table 2: Trends in Time Spent Cooking for US adults from 1965–1966 to 2007–2008," National Center for Biotechnology Information, http://www.ncbi.nlm.nih.gov/pmc/articles/PMC3639863/table/T2/.

16 Joanne Guthrie, Biing-Hwan Lin, Abigail Okrent, and Richard Volpe, "Americans' Food Choices at Home and Away: How Do They Compare with Recommendations?" US Department of Agriculture Economic Research Service, February 21, 2013, https://www.ers.usda.gov/amber-waves/2013/february/americans-food-choices-at-home-and-away/.

17 "Do Fast Food Restaurants Contribute to Obesity?" National Bureau of Economic Research, http://www.nber.org/bah/2009no1/w14721.html.

18 Cynthia L. Ogden and Margaret D. Carroll, "Prevalence of Overweight, Obesity, and Extreme Obesity Among Adults: United States, Trends 1960–1962 through 2007–2008," Centers for Disease Control and Prevention National Center for Health Statistics, http://www.cdc.gov/nchs/data/hestat/obesity_adult_07_08/obesity_adult_07_08.htm.

19 Amanda Marcotte, "Let's Stop Idealizing the Home-Cooked Family Dinner," *Slate*, September 3, 2014, http://www.slate.com/blogs/xx_factor/2014/09/03/home_cooked_family_dinners_a_major_burden_for_working_mothers.html.

20 Michael Pollan, *Cooked: A Natural History of Transformation* (New York: Penguin, 2013).

21 Johns Hopkins University Bloomberg School of Public Health, "Home Cooking a Main Ingredient in Healthier Diet, Study Shows," *ScienceDaily*, November 17, 2014.

22 Kiera Butler, "Weeknight Dinner 2.0," Natural Resources Defense Council, April 21, 2015, https://www.nrdc.org/onearth/weeknight-dinner-20.

23 Mark Bittman, "The Truth about Home Cooking," *Time*, October 9, 2014, http://time.com/3483888/the-truth-about-home-cooking/.

24 J. Lu, C. Huet, and L. Dubé, "Emotional Reinforcement as a Protective Factor for Healthy Eating in Home Settings," *American Journal of Clinical Nutrition* 94, no. 1 (2011): 254–61.

25 Ibid.

26 "American Time Use Survey," Bureau of Labor Statistics, December 20, 2016, http://www.bls.gov/TUS/CHARTS/HOUSEHOLD.HTM.

27 Thanks to Max Anderson for the Louis C.K., *Velveteen Rabbit*, and stone-smoothing analogies!

Conclusion

1   "Invasion of the Bottle Snatchers: Smaller Rivals Are Assaulting the World's Biggest Brands," *Economist*, July 9, 2016, http://www.economist .com/news/business/21701798-smaller-rivals-are-assaulting-worlds -biggest-brands-invasion-bottle-snatchers.

2   Hank Cardello, phone interview with the author, September 8, 2016.

3   Marion Nestle, phone interview with the author, April 14, 2015.

4   Michael Moss, phone interview with the author, September 7, 2016.

5   In his book *The Third Plate*, chef Dan Barber explores in much more detail how the farm-to-table movement came to be and what his philosophy and approach are for making food more sustainable.

6   Dan Wesser and Sean Naughton, "Another Grocery Store Headwind? Sizing Up the Meal Kit Market," *Piper Jaffray Industry Note*, June 13, 2016, https://www.forbes.com/sites/katiesola/2016/06/07/meal-kit-services -are-taking-a-bite-out-of-high-end-grocery-sales/.

7   Katie Sola, "Meal Kit Services Are Taking a Bite Out of High-End Grocery Sales," Forbes.com, June 7, 2016.

8   Alli Condra, "Why Fruits, Vegetables Are Excluded from Farm Subsidies," *Food Safety News*, November 9, 2011.

9   "Bitter Fruits," *Economist*.

10 This anecdote comes from a recent article on food inequality in "Bitter Fruits," *Economist*.

11 Julie A. Caswell and Ann L. Yaktine, *Supplemental Nutrition Assistance Program: Examining the Evidence to Define Benefit Adequacy* (Washington, D.C.: National Academies Press, 2013).

12 Vanessa Wong, "McDonald's Will Shift to Cage-Free Eggs by 2025," BuzzFeed, September 9, 2015.

13 Farmer and food activist Joel Salatin writes and speaks about "foodie elitism" from the farmer's perspective. You can read more about him and his farm at http://www.polyfacefarms.com/.